Cities and Territories of the Western Roman Empire

This book showcases the unique shape of urban development that took hold during the Roman Empire, beginning in the Mediterranean basin before spreading out across Europe, and offers a fresh perspective on the cities and territories of the Roman West.

With the expansion of Rome came a particular form of social organisation: the Roman city. This book provides a basic introduction to Roman cities, not through the lens of architecture and urbanism, but from a social, legal, cultural, spatial, and functional perspective. It focuses on the Roman *civitas* – the city and its territory – as the spatial model *par excellence* of Roman colonialism and expansion. Exploring primarily the cities and territories of the Western Empire, such as the Iberian Peninsula, Gaul, and Britain, González-Villaescusa revives from their ruins those central places that facilitated the circulation of people, goods, and information, forming the large urban network of a unified imperial territory.

Cities and Territories of the Western Roman Empire: 4th Century BC to the 3rd Century AD is suitable for school and university students, as well as the general reader interested in the subject of Roman cities in the Western Empire.

Ricardo González-Villaescusa is a former member of the School of Higher Hispanic Studies at Casa de Velázquez; he worked as a full professor at the universities of Reims – Champagne Ardenne, and Nice-Sophia Antipolis (France). Since 2019, he has been Professor of Archaeology in the Gaul and North-West Europe and member of UMR 7041 ArScAn – Archaeology and Sciences for Antiquity.

Cities and Territories of the Western Roman Empire
4th Century BC to the
3rd Century AD

Ricardo González-Villaescusa

Translation by Christian Rigg

LONDON AND NEW YORK

Designed cover image: Stefano Ravera/Alamy Stock Photo

First published in English 2024
by Routledge
4 Park Square, Milton Park, Abingdon, Oxon OX14 4RN

and by Routledge
605 Third Avenue, New York, NY 10158

Routledge is an imprint of the Taylor & Francis Group, an informa business

English translation © 2024 Ricardo González-Villaescusa

The right of Ricardo González-Villaescusa to be identified as author of this work has been asserted in accordance with sections 77 and 78 of the Copyright, Designs and Patents Act 1988.

All rights reserved. No part of this book may be reprinted or reproduced or utilised in any form or by any electronic, mechanical, or other means, now known or hereafter invented, including photocopying and recording, or in any information storage or retrieval system, without permission in writing from the publishers.

Trademark notice: Product or corporate names may be trademarks or registered trademarks, and are used only for identification and explanation without intent to infringe.

First published in French 2021 as *Les Cités romaines* by Que sais-je ?/Humensis

Les Cités romaines © Que sais-je?/Humensis, 2021

British Library Cataloguing-in-Publication Data
A catalogue record for this book is available from the British Library

ISBN: 978-1-032-58625-0 (hbk)
ISBN: 978-1-032-58626-7 (pbk)
ISBN: 978-1-003-45085-6 (ebk)

DOI: 10.4324/9781003450856

Typeset in Times New Roman
by Apex CoVantage, LLC

Contents

List of Figures vii
Author's Foreword ix
Preface to the English Edition xiii

Introduction 1

1 From City-State to Empire 9

2 The Western Territories of Roman Expansion 19

3 The Colonial Myth 32

4 The Empire's Urban Relays 45

5 Economic Autonomy 59

6 The City and Its Spaces 68

7 Life and Death in the City 78

Epilogue: The End of the *Civitas* 87

Index 95

Figures

0.1	Tabula Peutingeriana, 1st to 4th century CE. Facsimile edition by Konrad Miller, 1887/1888. Segments V, 3–5 and VI, 1–2.	2
2.1	The Western Roman Empire, its provinces and provincial capitals. Cities mentioned in-text.	20
2.2	Network of principal towns and main roads in *Hispania*.	22
2.3	Network of principal towns and main roads in Gaul.	26
2.4	Network of principal towns and main roads in *Britannia*.	28
3.1	Centuriations of *Arausio* (Orange).	38
3.2	Centuriation of the territory around the city *Aeso* (Isona, Spain), in divisions of 15 × 15 *actus*, with distribution of rural agricultural settlements.	39
4.1	Network of principal towns in Belgian Gaul, superimposed on the province's *civitates*, showing the hierarchy of primary and secondary settlements.	46
4.2	Network of towns in the *civitas* of Remi, including its capital of *Durocortorum* (Reims) and secondary settlements.	47
4.3	The Western Empire's main cities, Mediterranean ports (those cited more than three times by ancient sources), certain important ports of the Atlantic Ocean, as well as main roads and shipping routes.	49
4.4	Network of principal towns and main roads in *Hispania, Gallia, Germania*, and *Britannia*.	51
6.1	Roman city of *Tarraco* and main monuments: 1: Temple of Augustus, 2: Provincial Forum, 3: Circus, 4: Amphitheatre, 5: Public Baths, 6: Dwelling, 7: Walls, 8: Capitol, 9: Republican Forum, 10: Judicial Basilica; 11: Augustan Forum, 12: Open Commercial Area, 13: Theater, 14: Porticus post scaenam, 15: Nymphaeum, 16: Port Baths, 17: Warehouses (*horrea*), 18: Dock, 19: Pier on piles.	71

Author's Foreword

Not much time has passed between the publication of the original French edition of this book and this one, and there's little of great significance that differentiates them. Nonetheless, there are some changes that bear mentioning, and it's always useful to explain the context surrounding the publication of a book into a new language.

The well-known editorial series, *Que sais-je?* ('What do I know?'; University Press of France), served as an ideal format for the first edition. However, the maximum length of 200,000 characters did mean that every word had to be scrupulously 'weighed'.

As a consequence, citations throughout the 2021 text were limited to the bare minimum, and the bibliography at the end counts just 37 works. I hope the authors concerned can forgive me for these omissions. For the English edition, it was possible to include a full bibliography at the end of each chapter, totaling some 150 references. These contain both works cited and recommended readings. In other words: the principal works that have allowed me to accumulate, over the years, all the facts and knowledge presented here. Readers will also find newer works, published between the spring of 2021 and the autumn of 2023.

Likewise, whereas only two images made it into the 2021 edition, this one contains 12. Most of them complement and develop on Figure 2 from 2021. For example, new research into the ancient cities of the Iberian Peninsula has allowed us to double the total number of data points appearing in J. W. Hanson's 2016 synthesis. The goal is to provide a fuller picture of the spatial phenomena that underpin the central arguments set forth in this book. One of these arguments explores the idea of ancient Roman cities as nodes in a network, permitting the circulation of goods, people, and information, and how their density and position varied with geography (Figures 2.1, 2.2, 2.3, 2.4, 3.1, 3.2,

4.1, 4.2, 4.3). Another looks at how cities influenced the structure and organisation of their territories through the management of land and agricultural spaces. Figure 3.1, for example, shows a cadastre of the ancient colony of *Arausio* (Orange, France) and demonstrates the practice of centuriation – one of the several different ways land was divided up in the immense space occupied by the colonies and cities under Latin law in the Rhône Valley. A much different approach is taken in Figure 3.2, owing to the significantly smaller size of the municipality of *Aeso* and its territory in the Pyrenean foothills. Finally, Figure 6.1 shows the spatial and architectural organisation of *Tarraco*, an important provincial capital in ancient *Hispania* (reproduced here with the generous permission of its authors).

This latest edition was made possible thanks to the generous support of the Alliance EDUC (European Digital UniverCity), of which my university is a member, who funded the translation within the context of a course I teach on the Reception of Roman Urbanism in the Western Provinces of the Roman Empire.

My thanks go again to all those mentioned in the original edition of this book. I would also like to take this opportunity to thank Philippe Leveau for his preface to the English edition; Christian Rigg for the diligence and care he brought to translating the original French edition to English; and my partner, Esther Vidal-Ros, responsible for "translating" my spatial arguments into publishable illustrations (signed EOX) over the past 20 years.

Paris, Autumn 2023

Preface to the English Edition

In the introduction to this book, Ricardo González-Villaescusa gives a clear account of his objective: namely, to showcase the unique shape of urban development that appeared within the Mediterranean basin during the first three centuries of the Roman Empire.

To understand the importance of this exposé, it bears examining a word that historians of antiquity have used to designate all kinds of urban forms: the 'City'. Both the Greek word *polis* and the Latin word *civitas* are translated as such – and while this is true in a certain sense, *poleis* were much more than cities; they were true political states unto themselves. They existed at a time in the history of the rural development of Greek settlements when one's affiliation with a particular social group functioned independently of one's place of residence. And when Aristotle thought of the *polis* in the 4th century – at which time the language made a clear distinction between an *astu* or urban settlement and a *komé* or village – it was this he thought of. Reflecting on Plato's *Laws*, for example, Aristotle highlights the fact that satisfying the daily needs of 5,000 warriors, their wives and servants required the exploitation of immense tracts of land.

But the City is a historical entity. Our dictionaries teach us that the word 'City' comes from the Latin word *civitas* – a word that carries with it the legal concept we know today as *citizenship*. Intimately connected with the concept of the *res publica*, a *civitas* designated a group of citizens that shared the same rights and responsibilities. The conquering Romans used the term to refer to the peoples they subjugated and upon whom they imposed a model of habitation founded on the principles of the City. By the end of Antiquity, *civitas* came to represent a kind of idealised sociopolitical and spatial configuration, used by Augustus to question the fate of Rome in his defence of the city's new religion, where he contrasted the City of God with those of men.

Colonisation during the Republican era consisted of seeding a territory with colonies of citizens. As a result, the Empire's cities effectively served as provincial extensions of Rome, where local elites shared the power with those of the Eternal City. Connected by a dense network of roads and waterways, they reproduced all the aristocratic institutions characteristic of the Roman model, and each controlled a territory that brought together diverse populations, not all of whom were peasants. Some lived on estates (*villae*), others in settlements as diverse in name – *oppida, castella, fora, vici, conciliabula* – as in status and function. This type of City, or *civitas*, was fundamentally different from those that would come to exist when Constantine revived the Empire and moved its centre to Byzantium. The capital of a *civitas* retained its territorial preeminence – but the elites, more and more, retired to their countryside estates.

Exploring the historiography of the concept of the "Ancient City", H. Bruhns highlights the importance of history itself. Where the Greeks were concerned, early *polies* disposed of an important degree of autonomy, one justifying their qualification in English as "city-states"; *cités-État* in French and *Stadtstaaten* in German. They lost this quality during the age of the Hellenistic monarchies, and Roman emperors presented themselves as great liberators, returning to them their stolen freedoms.

To conceptualise Roman *civitates* as their own unique *ideal-type*, chronologically distinct from that of the Greek *polis*, González-Villaescusa is justified in his methodological choice to focus on the West, where the City undertook a new shape. And in doing so, the author reconnects with a debate on the ancient City that has divided anthropologists and historians alike.

One historian of particular note in this debate is M. I. Finley. In an article entitled *The Ancient City: From Fustel de Coulanges to Max Weber and beyond*, Finley offers a comprehensive account of the subject's historiography, its treatment by sociologists and anthropologists, and underscores the unique nature of Greco-Roman cities, typologically distinct from those of the East and the Middle Ages. Like Weber and the medievalist W. Sombart, he underscores the important interplay of politics and economics and defines the ancient City as fundamentally consumptive in nature – one which lives off of and draws from the countryside. Just as the empire derived its strength from the wealth of its provinces, the Roman city derived its sustenance from peasant labour. This notion was later adopted by Ch. Goudineau in his urban history of France in the early 1980s. Speaking to the economic functions of the "Cities of the *Pax romana*", Goudineau highlights a transformation in the City's economic dynamics following Roman conquest – one which inverted the relationship between protohistoric settlements and their territories. Thirty years later, though, scholars of the ancient City revisited this perspective within the framework of a History of urban Europe, questioning its characterisation as 'economically parasitic; a city which lives off the wealth of its province without producing anything, save for a few items it keeps for itself'.

Finley didn't have access to the insights from spatial archaeology that we possess today – insights which grew at a considerable pace once archaeologists moved out of cities to explore their territories. This spatial approach to the territory allows for a better understanding of the dynamics of urban and rural fabrics and restores to the ancient city the structuring role it played in the configuration and evolution of the *civitas* – that is, of the City and its territory – in the first three centuries of the Roman Empire. Ricardo González-Villaescusa offers a fresh, historically grounded perspective on this approach.

Emeritus Professor
of the University of Aix-Marseille
Centre Camille Jullian

Bibliography

Bruhns, H., Cité antique (Historiographie de la), in J. Leclant (dir.), *Dictionnaire de l'Antiquité*, Paris, PUF, 2005, pp. 502–504.

Finley, M. I., The Ancient City: From Fustel de Coulanges to Max Weber and Beyond, *Comparative Studies in Society and History*, 19(3), 1977, pp. 305–327.

Goudineau, C., Les villes de la paix romaine, in P. A. Février, M. Fixot, C. Goudineau, V. Kruta, 1. *La Ville antique: Des origines au IXe siècle*, G. Duby (dir.), *Histoire de la France urbaine*, Paris, Seuil, 1980, pp. 233–391.

Lafon, X., Marc, J. Y., Sartre, M., *La ville antique*, in J. L. Pinol (dir.), *Histoire de l'Europe urbaine*, Paris, Éditions du Seuil, 2011 [Reedition].

Introduction

The oldest representation we have today of the Roman Empire is a 13th-century copy of the *Peutinger Table* (Figure 0.1).

One's first impression – some kind of roadmap or 'GPS' of the ancient world? – quickly resolves into a series of distinctive elements. The section containing Rome, for example, markedly different from the segment containing *Cupra Marittima*, demonstrates a clear hierarchy between the cities, villages, and various way stations that adorn its roadways. The letters RO and MA straddle the figure of an emperor seated atop a throne and holding the globe and sceptre that symbolise his authority. Radiating outwards from the Eternal City are the 12 roads that linked Rome to Italy and the rest of the world. These include the *Viae Appia, Flaminia,* and *Aurelia*, as well as the *Via Ostiensis*, connecting it to Ostia at the mouth of the Tiber and the important maritime installations that existed there. The river, indeed all the rivers, blend and merge with the sea, while the shores of the Mediterranean lie dotted with coastal cities, ports, and representations of anchorages, warehouses, and the lighthouses of Alexandria and the Bosporus.

The great network of Roman roads appears as a series of red lines, segmented into individual stages by subtle indentations and figures that give the distance in miles, leagues, and parasangs between the more than 4000 toponyms, of which roughly 500 represent cities. These roads snake about, run along, and traverse mountain ranges, lakes, forests, deserts, and even the Nile delta. The western-most section is lost to us, but in its entirety, the *Tabula* would have measured more than seven metres in length. What remains represents approximately 8,000 kilometres of the *oecumene*, the inhabited world, stretching from the English Channel to India. Encompassing not only the Roman Empire itself but also a portion of China, it represents what

DOI: 10.4324/9781003450856-1

2 *Introduction*

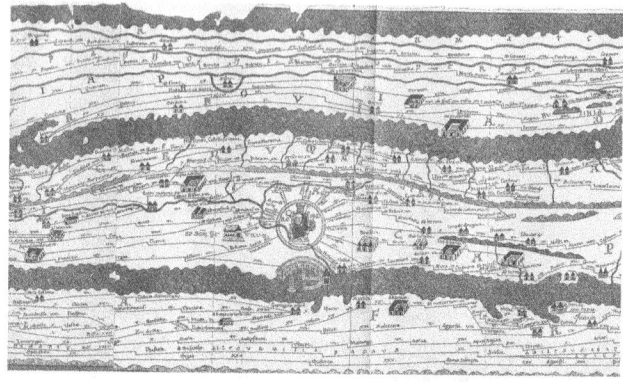

Figure 0.1 Tabula Peutingeriana, 1st to 4th century CE. Facsimile edition by Konrad Miller, 1887/1888. Segments V, 3–5 and VI, 1–2.
Source: www.doria.fi/handle/10024/90222. Wikidata: Q108512.

might be called today Rome's 'sphere of influence', or more simply, 'the Roman world'.

In truth, the *tabula* is a highly idealised representation of the Roman Empire, which saw itself as more homogenous, more spatially and territorially continuous than it really was. The distances inscribed on the map are intended to give a sense of the time required to travel the different stages of the *cursus publicus* (or *vehiculatio*), i.e., the official postal service. A wide array of interconnected infrastructural elements, including maritime and terrestrial routes, bridges, ports, lighthouses, relays, and cities, served to 'reduce' these distances, enabling those who travelled them to overcome the physical obstacles that would have otherwise made their journey impossible.

The responsibility for maintaining the *cursus publicus* (including its roads and relays, personnel, and beasts of burden) fell to the individual imperial cities. Collectively, they oversaw whatever infrastructure passed through their region, facilitating communications throughout the empire. This desire to simplify travel and transportation likewise informed the spatial relationships between cities and their territories, most notably through the roadways that not only connected urban spaces with their respective territories but also played a crucial role in structuring and defining those spaces. The land surveyor Hyginus

Gromaticus, for example, advocated for a precise proportionality between the routes that connected a city to its territory. Each city was embedded within the same axial system and orientation as the rest of its territory and, ultimately, the world. As a result, the empire's inhabitants, regardless of their place of residence, participated in a single, common spatiality – albeit one which evolved over time. In this way, the empire's cities and territories shared with Rome and its empire an important 'relation' of spatial interdependence. This 'ideology of centrality' of the Roman world, to borrow a term from N. Purcell, was both a cause and an effect of the accumulation of social, economic, and civic activities and functions within Roman cities, which in turn promoted the circulation of individuals, information, and goods.

The Roman Empire's distinct spatial configuration, mottled with spatial discontinuity, punctuated by geographic and social enclaves, and demonstrating a variety of spatial realities at different scales, was the result of a dynamic period of productivity that spanned three centuries. This 'Roman space' was shared by colonies of Roman citizens (situated sometimes thousands of kilometres from Rome); various urban agglomerations, including *vici*; urbanised villages; loci of commercial exchange, such as *fora*; hamlets and isolated farms, bound inevitably to some nearby city; autonomous Greek *poleis*; *municipia*; and myriad other spatial realities, each of which held a specific civic status and contributed to the apparent continuity of the Empire as we see it today on *Peutinger's Table*.

The goal of this book is not to provide a historical account of Roman colonisation or the urbanisation of the Roman Empire. Instead, its focus is the Roman *civitas*[1] – the city and its territory – as the spatial model *par excellence* of Roman colonialism. The term 'colonialism' is used here in much the same way as it was by contemporaneous historians, to encompass not only the foundation of Roman and Latin colonies but also the broader expansion of Roman power, the *imperium*, and how this expansion influenced the organisation of territories incorporated into the empire. It was a process that began with complex, discontinuous, even clumsy territorial arrangements but which evolved to include more stable and homogeneous configurations from the 1st century AD onward. 'Roman colonialism' took on a variety of forms over the years: the incorporation of territories into the empire, sometimes accompanied by the appearance of Roman settler colonies; Latin colonies (of settlers from Latium); the appropriation and refoundation of native cities; and the promotion of pre-existing cities to important new statuses. Each such process resulted in the integration (or creation) of a spatial 'cell' or 'unit': the Roman *civitas*, meaning the city and its territory, incorporated one by one into imperial territory. Thus, rather than a heterogenous assembly of disparate territories, the Empire saw itself as a unified imperial territory, organised about a single political centre.

Roman cities comprised both a social component – the *civitas*, i.e., the city and its territory – and a physical and spatial component – the *urbs* or city proper. Understanding them fully means mobilising both historical and archaeology perspectives as well as certain principles of geography (such as metropolitanism, discontinuous urbanisation, topography, topology, and networks). Both historical and archaeological sources show that the Roman *civitas* was a civil and political centre, a space where a wide variety of human activity was concentrated and which behaved as a kind of social hub.

Our study begins in those critical decades leading up to the Augustinian monarchy, after the crisis of the Social War and, in 89 BC, the granting of Roman citizenship to all free men living in Italy – a law which only came into full effect following the censorships of 70–69 and 28 BC, after which time these citizens enjoyed a kind of dual citizenship (that of their city of origin and that of Rome). It was a period of great tension between the ever-expanding city-state of Rome and the other Italian cities who didn't benefit equally from Rome's conquests. The solution was to dissociate Roman citizenship from actual residency within the city. With this done, the cities in question became extensions of Rome and their inhabitants, by the same coin, subjects of the Empire. But this posed another problem: just who among the newly integrated populations was a 'Roman citizen' and who was not? Spatiality played an important role in answering this question. The newly incorporated peoples and territories were grouped and regrouped into *civitates* and provinces, settled or made to settle in existing or newly founded cities. Traditional territorial hierarchies were overthrown. In their place appeared new configurations (albeit ones that drew extensively on existing networks) that allowed the Romans to more effectively appropriate the territories of neighbouring populations and incorporate them as natural extensions of Rome, participant in the shared Roman fiction of temporal and spatial continuity.

Of course, territorial continuities (and discontinuities) were reflected in the attribution of political and social rights. But what were these rights that Italy's elites had so coveted? At the individual level, they included the *conubium* (the right to marriage), *commercium* (the ability to sign contracts and the right to buy and sell goods), and the *provocatio* (the right to appeal to the general public in cases of heavy fines or capital punishment). At the public level: suffrage and the right to run for office, according to one's wealth as recorded in the *census*. In other words, the right to participate in political life. With these new rights, Italian, Hispanic, Gallic, and African elites adopted Roman customs and practices and even gained access to the Roman *cursus honorum* and the consulate. All of this was the culmination of a process begun three generations earlier and which ended with the transformation of the city-state of Rome into the *caput mundi*: 'capital of the world'.

The military, judicial, and political systems employed in the conquest, expropriation, and administration of these distant spaces would have been of little use if they hadn't been connected to one another by maritime, riverine, and terrestrial transportation as part of a robust network of communications and, as mentioned earlier, spatial continuity. (This was especially true of Gaul, where there existed myriad points of convergence and infrastructural developments both large and small.) The different cities and territories depended heavily on the roads and relays that appeared alongside these new administrative divisions and 'centres of power', many of which brought together diverse populations in a single *civitas* comprising a principal city and its surrounding region. Existing urban spaces grew denser with the arrival of the Romans, who altered or added to them, reorganising the space according to their own geopolitical interests. In cases of insufficient urbanisation or infrastructure, Rome established new urban centres in close proximity to existing settlements, taking into account existing spatial realities (such as a port, a well-established trading post, or some strategic crossroad), the distances between them, and the available means of travel (such as horses and marching armies). And all of it was organised around those autonomous units that were the *civitates*, both a consequence of and a contributor to the social and civil organisation of Roman society.

In 212 AD, the emperor Caracalla granted full Roman citizenship – and thus access to political life – to all free men in the Empire. This 'generalised citizenship' contributed to the greater level of urbanisation one sees from the 3rd century onward. But this period of prosperity for Roman cities, whose expansion had not ceased since 70 BC, ended in 330 AD with the foundation of the city that was to replace Rome: Constantinople, the 'Rome of the East'. It was both a symptom and a symbol of the great territorial upheaval that beset the empire at this time and the reorganisation of the urban hierarchy that followed it. The dominant model of antiquity, that of the *polis-civitas*, was soon thereafter replaced.

The pages that follow focus primarily on the West, with a few notable excursions into the East, including Egypt and Greece, where the spatial model of the *civitas* existed for many centuries and was the most widespread of such models following the death of Alexander the Great. That said, the status of *municipium* and Latin law more generally was never met with the same enthusiasm in the East as in the West. Indeed, as a status reserved for the inhabitants of Roman colonies, Roman citizenship was far less common in the East. (Greek *poleis* were integrated but remained autonomous, albeit not entirely independent from Rome.) Rather, it was in the West, at the furthest reaches of its empire, that Rome's influence as a vector for the propagation of the spatial model of the *polis-civitas* was most strongly felt and where a whole host of civic statuses (from Latin colonies to *municipia* and so-called 'titular colonies') were invented to facilitate access to citizenship and integrate a large number of local elites. Roman expansion into these territories, already dotted with communities approximating *civitates*, accelerated the 'polisization'[2] and urbanisation of the Iberian Peninsula, Gaul, and of course Britain, where the Roman conquest brought about changes similar to those the Romans themselves and other Mediterranean populations had already experienced.

Cicero described these colonies as *propugnacula imperii* (*Lege Agraria*, II, 73), bastions of the empire or 'outposts of (imperial) power'. Together, the *civitas* and the *urbs* served as a vector of 'civilization', to borrow a concept from Joseph Conrad's 1896 short story *An Outpost of Progress*, where, in a tiny, far-flung African trading post of the Great Trading Company, the character known as Carlier, dreaming aloud one night, turns to his colleague Kayerts and muses: 'In a hundred years, there will be perhaps a town here. Quays, and warehouses, and barracks, and – and – billiard-rooms. Civilisation, my boy, and virtue – and all.'

* * *

Despite its necessarily reduced length, this book[3] is the result of work conducted in Reims while preparing a course on cities in Belgic Gaul. Later, in Nice, I adapted this approach to Gallia Narbonensis and the Alpine provinces. Once in Nanterre, I returned my focus to the North and the British Isles as part of a third-year seminar covering the great Roman adventure that was the diffusion of the city to the western-most reaches of its empire. The common thread in these investigations was a spatial one, a geographical reading of the Roman world, with the goal of answering one deceptively simple question: why here, and not somewhere else? When faced with this same question, the authors of antiquity answered with 'providence' – the *pronoia* of the stoics that permeates ancient texts and saw physical environments as a boon, granted to humans to settle and, in this case, build cities. This concept lent its name to the *Pronoïa* project that served as a framework for a series of seminars given at the University of Nice and which led to two international conferences in Antibes (*Rencontre Internationales d'Archéologie et d'Histoire d'Antibes*) and the resulting publications: *Implantations humaines en milieu littoral méditerranéen* (Human Settlements in the Mediterranean Coastal Environment; 2014) and *L'Exploitation des ressources maritimes de l'Antiquité* (Exploitation of Maritime Resources in Antiquity; 2017), as well as a series of eponymous digs financed first by the *Fondation Unice* and later the UCA.

A three-month sojourn undertaken in 2016, thanks to support from the INSHS and the *Casa de Velázquez* for the project *Les formes de l'habitat groupé de l'Occident romain* (Forms of Clustered Settlements in the Roman West), allowed me to continue this work. This was succeeded by a multi-year program at the *Casa de Velázquez* entitled *L'habitat groupé en Méditerranée occidentale: IIe siècle av. J.-C. – IIIe siècle apr. J.-C.* (Clustered Settlements in the Western Mediterranean: 1st century BC – 2nd century AD). Finally, generous support from the Roman Islam Center for Comparative Empire and Transcultural Studies (University of Hamburg) and the German Research Foundation (DFG) allowed me to complete this work in the context of the project *Cités des confins de l'Empire romain ou Comment gouverner la périphérie* (Cities at the Edge of the Roman Empire, or How to Govern the Periphery.)

* * *

Notes

1 Translator's Note: In the original French text, the author draws a distinction between the terms 'ville' (city) and 'cité' (Latin *ciuitas*, pl. *ciuitates*). While the former readily translates to 'city' and the

two are essentially synonymous, 'cité' carries the meaning of 'a historically, politically, or socially cohesive assembly' and, particularly in antiquity, refers to a self-organised political community. Aside from 'city', the other conventional translation for 'cité' is 'city-state'. But when applied to this period, the term suggests a higher degree of autonomy than actually existed. Each city was attached to a territory and responsible for its maintenance and governance, but they were nonetheless subservient to Rome and part of its empire. For this reason, the Latin 'civitas' is used in place of 'cité', and, on occasion, 'a city and its territory' for greater clarity.
2 Diffusion and adoption of the Greco-Roman *polis* or *civitas* model. It is preferable to its Latin equivalent, 'civilisation', laden with ethnocentric connotations.
3 This book, and any errors it may contain, are the sole responsibility of the author. I would, however, like to express my sincere gratitude to the following individuals, who offered corrections and insights: Frédéric Gayet, Michel Tarpin, Gérard Chouquer, and Patrick Le Roux.

Bibliography

Guillaumin, J. Y., *Les Arpenteurs romains. Tome I: Hygin le gromatique – Frontin*, Paris, Les Belles Lettres, 2005.

Hansen, M. H., *Polis. Une introduction à la cité grecque*, Paris, Les Belles Lettres, 2008.

Purcell, N., Urban Spaces and Central Places, in S. E. Alcock, R. Osborne (dir.), *Classical Archaeology*, Oxford, Blackwell, 2007, pp. 182–202.

1 From City-State to Empire

1 Founding and Building a City

It hardly seems possible to speak of Roman cities without first evoking the mythical foundation of Rome. Myths serve two purposes. First, they constitute an important point of reference for the ever-evolving societies that identify with them. In the case of Rome, the myth of Romulus and Remus describes how the city first came into existence. Second, the performative nature of myths confers upon them a universal validity: by harking back to some ancestral success story, myths encourage their own diffusion and legitimise changes in the society.

B. Liou-Gille showed how the myth of Rome's foundation explores the essential components for establishing any urban settlement, consisting not just of a city but also a community. This well-known myth, recounted by authors like Titus Livius and Dionysius of Halicarnassus, highlights key factors in forming a socially and politically organised group, including norms, gathering places, and organisations. These can be broken down into 10 steps: (1) selecting the founders (Romulus and Remus); (2) selecting the location and space (the *sulcus primigenius* and the *Roma quadrata*); (3) obtaining favour from the gods (*auspices*); (4) giving the city a name, preferably one tied to its founder (*Roma*); (5) establishing the city limits (by tracing a line in the soil with a plough, thus marking the outline of the future ramparts); (6) erecting city walls (to protect and limit access to the interior space); (7) creating meeting spaces (e.g. the *Campus Martius*, the *Curia*, the *forum*) for each of the various groups of citizens (the *populus*, the *patres*, the *quirites*, etc.); (8) promoting social cohesion with the inauguration of a central space (*mundus*) where divine offerings can be made to the subterranean gods; (9) organising the society (e.g., three tribes and 30 *curiae*); and (10) establishing communal norms (the Laws of the 12 Tables).

DOI: 10.4324/9781003450856-2

Four of these criteria relate to social and politico-religious cohesion: choosing the founders, obtaining favour from the gods, choosing a name, and establishing laws and a social structure. Four others are of a spatial nature: the choice of a location, delimitation of the urban space, erection of the walls, and the construction of meeting spaces and civic centres. Finally, one element can be characterised as a mix of the two: the promotion of social ties with the creation of a pit, the *mundus*, placed at the centre of the city and the meeting point of the axes of the *Roma quadrata*. This balance reflects the desire to form a civic community in a suitable space and within a specific framework.

The city, as focal point of the territory or *ager*, served as the seat of the ensemble's legal authority: the *civitas*, whose authority extended throughout the territory. The nature of this legal authority is well illustrated by the mythological foundation of Rome and its delimitation in space by the *pomœrium*. Indeed, Remus is sentenced to death for having crossed, even in jest, the furrow defining the city's limits! Location, jurisdiction, access to the city's interior, the existence and protection of spaces where political decisions are made – all were essential aspects of Roman cities.

By ensuring that the foundation of future cities adhered to a simplified version of this myth, the Empire contributed to the rise of a certain type of urban civilisation. This 'spatial utopia', as a result of the essential steps leading to the creation of a new city and the delimitation of the space necessary for the creation of a new community of citizens, lent itself to a specific spatial representation. The myth of Rome's foundation, as well as the works of Vitruvius and ancient surveyors, demonstrates that Roman society aspired to a certain level of spatial continuity. The goal was to anchor the city within its territory, connected to other cities, within a harmonious universe.

2 The First Roman Colonies

The first Roman colonies precede by two or three centuries our main period of focus. Nonetheless, it bears briefly examining Rome's earliest colonial efforts, from the 4th to the 1st centuries BC, to better understand Rome's territorial policies once it became a city at the head of an empire and the *ager romanus* was made to extend beyond the boundaries of Rome and Italy.

These policies were applied in two successive ways. The first consisted of creating new, extraterritorial urban projections that extended outward from Rome itself, under its direction and settled by Roman colonists and their families. The goal of this was mainly defensive: establishing a Roman presence at some strategic location (often coastal, to defend against attacks by sea). An outpost, as it were. They were similar in function to the Greek *epiteichismata*: far-flung strongholds such as Massalia on the southern coast of Gaul (modern-day Marseille). The Greek term, incidentally, is very close to the term used by Cicero for such Roman colonies, *propugnacula imperii*. Roman colonies during this time resembled Greek bastions in their configuration and the geometry of their internal space: a quadrangular form, protected by ramparts, with perpendicular axes extending inward from the city gates and dividing the internal space into lots of equal dimensions. This configuration borrowed from the principles of regularity that Aristotle noted were popular at the time: 'after the modern fashion, that is, the one introduced by Hippodamus' (Politics, 7, 11, 1330a). It can be found in the so-called *coloniae maritimae* or 'maritime colonies' (such as Ostia, Terracina, Minturno, and Pozzuoli), albeit without public or state buildings, for the simple reason that such colonies lacked autonomy and hosted only smaller contingents of colonists (300) that occupied lots of a limited size (2 *jugers* or 2,520 square metres).

The second manner was employed both later (in the 3rd and 2nd centuries BC) and further from Rome. In this case, Romans founded autonomous cities, either *ex nihilo* on virgin soil or by expelling a local population and expropriating the existing infrastructure (e.g., Cosa and Luni). Buildings were erected or repurposed to lodge the new inhabitants and serve their purposes. In the latter case, this process implied the juridical, political, and civic erasure (e.g., deportation or enslavement) of local populations.

As territories were conquered and extended, the annihilation of existing communities became less frequent – not for reasons of humanity but rather of pragmatism or 'rational imperialist political choice' (in the words of M. Tarpin). That is, to avoid depopulation. Through a series of specific provisions and clauses, the very formal conditions of the *deditio* (surrender, submission, etc.) allowed for the conservation of local populations while ownership of the land was transferred to Rome. In such cases, the inhabitants who were permitted to remain in place and continue working the land did so in exchange for a *vectigal* or land tax. The Roman State was also known to dispense land strategically, giving it to supporters of Rome and withholding it from dissidents. The alternative, so-called 'scorched earth' policies, were susceptible to causing depopulation and thus interruptions in the nascent empirical urban network.

Land was also allocated on an individual basis (*viritim*) to citizens who were authorised to rent or otherwise acquire a portion of the newly incorporated land. Such attributions are less obvious in ancient texts than the large colonial capitulations mentioned earlier, though, and come to us primarily through archaeological and epigraphic sources.

This kind of 'soft' colonial appropriation wasn't without consequence for the territory. Rather than relocating Roman citizens *en masse* and monopolising the land, policies tended to prioritise the elevation or promotion of a local population to the rank of Latin colony (often as a reward for maintaining good relations with Rome). At the end of their mandate, individuals holding the position of magistrate became full Roman citizens. Bit by bit, *civitates peregrinae* – provinces and even entire groups of provinces (as was the case with *Hispania* during the reign of Vespasian; see Chapter 3) – were incorporated into the Roman empire (a process sometimes referred to as 'auto-Romanisation').

Free, indigenous cities, by grace of their existing relationship with Rome (e.g., Marseille) and federated cities (e.g., Cádiz) who sided with Rome during territorial confrontations maintained their autonomy. Only their foreign policy – that is, their relationship vis-à-vis other, non-Roman cities – was overseen by Rome, until such a time as they were properly and fully integrated into the empire and granted an appropriate territorial status.

3 Construction of the Provincial Territory

All the various approaches to territorial occupation employed by the Romans from the 1st century BC onward appeared in an experimental fashion before that. But the manner and degree to which they were applied to a territory when it finally submitted to the Empire differed according to a variety of geopolitical and ethnic factors. The occupation of the earliest provinces (such as Cisalpine Gaul, Transalpine Gaul, and *Hispania*) occurred in a less coordinated fashion, while conquests of the later provinces (e.g., *Britannia* and *Dacia*) were characterised by greater uniformity in terms of colonial tactics and legal status. That said, the existence of local urban traditions of varying longevity, the type of conquest – whether more or less combative – and the presence of pre-existing spatial realities and territorial configurations all led to the development of distinct regional outcomes.

P. Le Roux has shown how often *civitas* and *res publica* were more or less synonymous in *Hispania Baetica* and Africa and less so in the cities of *Gallia Narbonensis*.

This experiment, tying individuals to both their own cities and the promethean myth of the *imperium*, saw itself validated in the waning influence of Rome's more conservative attitudes during the Social War, whose causes and solution were territorial in nature. Rome's answer was to extend citizenship to neighbouring cities, whose citizens thus benefited from dual citizenship. Of course, it didn't take long for the social and political elites of the provinces to petition Rome for a similar outcome, and Roman citizenship was finally made universal in 212 AD under Caracalla.

Public religion also played an important role in the organisation of far-flung colonised territories and the nature of their inhabitants' dual identity. The work of J. Scheid and similar authors in the anthropological study of the Roman religion has helped demonstrate how a *civitas*' public religion helped structure its territory. The latter became a kind of 'religious landscape', tying together the various symbols of public worship, such as temples and chapels. Studies of the spaces occupied by religious practices in the urban fabric of Italic colonies along the Adriatic coast suggest the existence of unique colonial identities, based on local interpretations of the *Urbs*. Such identities reflect the preeminence of political power over religious influence that occurred towards the end of the Republic. This trend continued under the principate with the emergence of the imperial cult. At the same time, the imperial cult had a large impact on the infrastructure of cities and provinces. Take, for example, the erection of the Sanctuary of the Three Gauls (*Tres Galliae*) in Lyon; or that of the *ara Ubiorum* in Cologne, where Celtic and Germanic locals came together to worship Augustus and the goddess Roma; or else the great provincial forum of Tarragona, built to a similar end during the reign of Vespasian and which was inspired by similar Roman structures, in particular the forum of Augustus.

Thus, the empire's colonies and provincial capitals were characterised by a blending of religious and urban landscapes. Additionally, rural sanctuaries played an important role in organising the empire's urban spaces. For example, the *Sanctuaire de la Combe de l'Ermitage* ('Sanctuary of the Valley of the Hermitage') in Collias (Gard, France), built near a spring close to ancient Nîmes, allowed the populations of many adjacent towns to gather in worship of Jupiter, the emperor, and various other local divinities of the nearby *Coriobedenses* and *Budenicenses*.

In northern Gaul and the Germanic provinces, rural sanctuaries take on, in the words of P. Gros, 'the appearance of the city, even without fulfilling its functions'. Such spaces were separate from but closely tied to the city and could reach up to several hundred hectares in size. There's no doubt they played an important role in organising the territory. Some of these settlements were equipped not only with thermal baths (which makes sense, given their proximity to thermal springs) but also theatres and amphitheatres. Gisacum in Vieil-Évreux (Gaule), Bath (*Aquae sulis*) in the United Kingdom, and Faimingen (*Phoebiana*) in Germany are all examples.

The presence of such official sanctuaries and public baths helps demonstrate the efforts involved in binding the civic community around a common religious identity at various territorial levels (interprovincial, provincial, regional, and urban). These signs of public piety played an integral role in the empire's spatial continuity, 'filling in' the gaps in territorial infrastructure.

4 Colonial Law and Land Rights

The existing communities being incorporated into the empire, as well as the terms of the *deditio* (e.g. capitulation or surrender), could also influence how land was distributed. The destruction of a rampart was a common symbolic gesture to this end, representing the dissolution of the pre-existing civic community and, more importantly, transfer of the land to the victor. With distance and time, though, the appropriation of new lands necessitated the adoption of different practices, in line with the growing diversity of territorial statuses.

The sheer magnitude of Rome's colonial efforts, the evolution of Roman society itself, the diverse peoples and societies it encountered (each with their own laws and codes), and the interplay of Rome's highly stratified social structure with indigenous social hierarchies all prove just how difficult it is to offer a generic framework for the various legal solutions Rome adopted and imposed upon the peoples and lands it conquered. In a recent overview, G. Chouquer presents a kind of Code of Roman Agrarian Law, examining these options and their representation in Roman 'agrimensoric' law (that of Roman surveyors). These laws offer an important global perspective on why and how such solutions were used in the creation of a civic network or territorial continuum, as well as the critical role they played in the different 'agrarian conditions' (to borrow a term from the *agrimensores* themselves) and civic statuses of citizens and newly created cities.

Indeed, surveyors charged with zoning and planning the urban space had to adapt to a variety of local situations and developed a wide range of methods for managing the *ager publicus*. Beneath the surface of the apparent homogeneity of the 'Roman world' existed a complex multiplicity of systems of tenancy. These various spatial realities were codified by surveyors, and it is not uncommon to find written records that distinguish between one set of rights applied to a specific lot of land and another set of more general, universal rights.

Faced with such diversity, surveyors relied on a variety of tools to help them in their duties, especially with regards to metrology (e.g., conversion tables for local measurements). One principle, however, was universal: *dominium*. That is, 'the power that the authorities of Rome gave themselves to determine the fate of territories, lands, and their populations, according to their colonial policies'. This principle is reflected in the distinction surveyors made between 'being on Roman land' and 'being a Roman colony', both of which differed from provincial land policies imposed upon conquered territories.

The situation thus varied according to the attitudes adopted by conquered populations in regard to Rome, just as citizenship varied with land policies and status. None of this is to say that Rome formally recognised local laws. Rather, the mosaic of colonial laws it imposed on others was sufficiently broad to cover a variety of circumstances. Colonisation enabled the Romans to employ a variety of practices borrowed from their own community to provide structure for the diverse colonial conditions: colonies of many different types; prefectures, *municipia* and their various statuses; *vici, oppida, fora*, and *pagi, conciliabula, conventus civium Romanorum*, and *saltus*. The most important of these – and the differences between them – are outlined next.

Colonies, as we have seen, could serve as garrisons, settlements, or as host to new citizens. Maritime colonies, starting in the 4th century BC, served as coastal 'outposts', charged with defending the Empire from naval threats. They were guarded by just 300 citizens and so housed very few families. They weren't autonomous, but neither were they directly under Roman administration. As for settler colonies, these were organised in much the same way as *municipia* and bore many resemblances to Rome. Latin colonies of the 4th and 3rd centuries BC served the purpose of settler colonialism, and land was distributed by lots to thousands of settlers and their families. Some 3,000 to 5,000 settlers could receive anywhere from 75 to 125 square kilometres of workable land. Finally, Roman colonialism of the 1st century BC largely benefited veterans of the Social War and Roman civil wars.

From very early on, Latin Rights exclusively concerned colonies in the West, as this is where most Latin (i.e., relating to Latium, the region around the city of Rome, common to both Romans and Latins) settlements took root. Roman citizens who lived in such settlements forewent their original citizenship in favour of Latin citizenship. The first phase of this kind of colonialism was federal in nature: any new citizen could obtain full citizenship from any city in the federation, provided they gave up their former citizenship. And the common denominator among the various forms of Latin law? The rights granted collectively to communities, populations, and provinces. The *oppida* of Latin citizens and the *civitates* under Latin law in Gaul and Spain. Latin law continued to function in this manner under Flavian and up until Vespasian extended it in a general fashion to the cities of Spain in 73 and 74 AD. Citizens of these *municipia* enjoyed a variety of personal statuses, as evidenced by Hispanic municipal laws inscribed on bronze. Starting in 338 BC, the *municipia* began to replace federal colonialism. Rome, as a result, adjusted its colonial strategy in favour of one that allowed for greater autonomy (although a colony's foreign policies would still be dictated by Rome). Following the Social War, Latin cities became full-fledged *municipia*, while the non-Latin cities of Italy were granted citizenship (*sine suffragio*), thus becoming municipalities *sans* suffrage. *Praefectura* of the 4th and 3rd centuries consisted of territorial communities with administrative autonomy but without voting rights or magistrates who 'spoke the law' (*iure dicundo*). Geographically speaking, *praefecturae* could even take the shape of an enclave within the territory of some other colony (*in alienis finibus*).

The status of *oppidum* was granted to cities which were technically neither colonies nor *municipia*, while *fora* (smaller communities connected to cities or towns) served to accommodate colonists who purchased or acquired land on an individual (*viritim*) rather than collective basis. This latter situation is one of the most basic configurations of the *res publica* or 'civic life'. *Vici* (sing. *vicus*) were waystations overseeing the control of some resource or roadway; *pagi* (sing. *pagus*) were subdivisions within a public territory (in Africa, for example, there were *pagi* composed of veterans granted land and rights '*viritane*', or on an individual basis). A *castellum* was a small, detached fort or fortlet (and sometimes other small buildings associated with it) which housed Roman citizens and was typically located within the (private) territory of a local community. A *conciliabulum* can be described as a Roman administrative unit, dependent on a colony or other autonomous entity under the sole authority of Rome. Finally, a *conventus civium Romanorum* was a community of Roman citizens, frequently merchants, residing within a peregrine *civitas*.

Bibliography

Bandelli, G., La colonizzazione romana della Penisola Iberica da Scipione Africano a Bruto Callaico, in G. Urso (dir.), *Hispania terris omnibus felicior. Premesse ed esiti di un processo di integrazione*, Pisa, ETS, 2002, pp. 105–142.

Bats, M., Les colonies massaliètes de Gaule méridionale: Sources et modèles d'un urbanisme militaire aux IVe-IIIe s. av. J.-C., in *Des Ibères aux Vénètes. Phénomènes proto-urbains et urbains de l'Espagne à l'Italie du Nord (IVe – IIe s. av. J.-C.). Actes du colloque international de Rome (1999)*, Rome, École Française de Rome, 2004, pp. 51–64.

Beltrán Lloris, F., Les colonies latines d'Hispanie (IIe siècle av. n. È.): Émigration italique et intégration politique, in N. Barrandon, F. Kirbihler (dirs.), *Les gouverneurs et les provinciaux sous la République romaine*, Rennes, Presses Universitaires de Rennes, 2011, pp. 131–144.

Bertrand, A., Y-a-t-il un paysage religieux colonial? Entre prescription, mimétisme et adaptation: Les mécanismes de l'*imitatio Romae*, *Revue de l'histoire des religions*, 4, 2010, pp. 591–608.

Carandini, A., *Roma. Il primo giorno*, Roma – Bari, Laterza, 2007.

Chouquer, G., *Code de droit agraire romain. Référents antiques pour le pluralisme et les anciens régimes fonciers*, Paris, Publi-Topex, 2022.

Christol, M., Fiches, J. L., Rabay, D., Le sanctuaire de la Combe de l'Ermitage à Collias (Gard), *Revue archéologique de Narbonnaise*, 40, 2007, pp. 15–32.

Dondin-Payre, M., Raepsaet-Charlier, M. T. (dirs.), *Sanctuaires, pratiques cultuelles et territoires civiques dans l'Occident romain, Séminaire d'histoire romaine et d'épigraphie latine, Centre G. Glotz (UMR 8585: CNRS-Paris I-Paris IV-ÉPHÉ)*, Bruxelles, Le Livre Timperman, 2006.

Dondin-Payre, M., Raepsaet-Charlier, M. T. (dirs.), *Cités, municipes, colonies: Les processus de municipalisation en Gaule et en*

Germanie sous le Haut Empire romain, Nouvelle édition, Paris, Éditions de la Sorbonne, 2009.

García Garrido, M., Mangas Manjarrés, J., *La Lex Ursonensis*: Estudio y edición crítica, *Studia historica. Historia Antigua*, 15, Salamanca, Universidad de Salamanca, 1997.

Gros, P., La ville comme symbole. Le modèle central et ses limites, in H. Inglebert (dir.), *Histoire de la civilisation romaine*, Paris, Presses Universitaires de France, 2005, pp. 155–232.

Hermon, E., *La colonie romaine: Espace, territoire, paysage. Les Gromatici entre histoire et droit pour la gestion des ressources naturelles*, Besançon, Presses Universitaires de Franche-Comté, 2020.

Humbert, M., *Municipium et civitas sine suffragio. L'organisation de la conquête jusqu'à la guerre sociale*, Roma, École Française de Rome, 1977.

Le Roux, P., *Vicus* et *castellum* en Lusitanie sous l'Empire, in Actas del Coloquio Les campagnes de Lusitanie romaine: Occupation du sol et habitat), *Studia Historica. Historia antigua*, 10–11, 1992–1993 [1994], pp. 151–160.

Liou-Gille, B., La fondation de Rome: Lectures de la tradition, *Histoire Urbaine*, 13, 2005, pp. 67–83.

Ortiz-de-Urbina, E. (coord.), *Ciudadanías, Ciudades y Comunidades cívicas en Hispania (de los Flavios a los Severos)*, Sevilla, Universidad de Sevilla, 2019.

Polignac, F. de, Scheid, J. (dirs.), Avant-propos. Qu'est-ce qu'un "paysage religieux". Représentations cultuelles de l'espace dans les sociétés anciennes, *Revue de l'histoire des religions*, 4, 2010, pp. 427–434.

Reddé, M., Dubois, L., Briquel, D., Lavagne, H., Queyrel, F. (eds.), *La naissance de la ville Antique*, Paris, De Boccard, 2003.

Tarpin, M., L'appropriation du territoire par Rome: Conquête, *deditio, foedus*, confiscation, in M. Aberson, M. C. Biella, M. di Fazio, P. Sanchez, M. Wullschleger (eds.), *L'Italia centrale e la creazione di una koiné culturale? I Percorsi della "romanizzazione"*, Genève, Peter Lang, 2016, pp. 183–193.

Tarpin, M., *Urbem condere/coloniam deducere*: La procédure de "fondation" coloniale, dans, in M. Tarpin (dir.), *Colonies, territoires et statuts: Nouvelles approches*, Suppléments aux *Dialogues d'Histoire Ancienne*, 23, 2021, pp. 13–94.

Zanker, P., The City as Symbol: Rome and the Creation of an Urban Image (in E. Fentress (ed.), *Romanization and the City: Creation, Transformations and Failures*), Portsmouth, *Journal of Roman Archaeology Supplement*, 38, 2000, pp. 25–41.

2 The Western Territories of Roman Expansion

Among the various factors that influenced how the Roman model was applied to different territories, the existing cultures of local populations was an important one. It also depended on the precise moment at which that integration took place. This chapter examines the cultural legacy left by those who were subsumed into the empire and how Rome adapted to them over time and in different regions of the Roman West (i.e., the Iberian Peninsula; North Africa; Gaul, including *Gallia Narbonensis*, *Tres Galliae*, and the Germanies; and Britain). Indeed, Roman territorial policies changed significantly during the 300 years that separated the first occupation of *Hispania* in the 3rd century BC and that of the British Isles in the middle of the 1st century AD and the last of the settlements founded by Trajan veterans in Africa Proconsularis, *Thamugadi* (Timgad, Algeria). Even within these territories, homogeneity was hardly the norm. The northwest of the Iberian Peninsula most closely resembled the north of Gaul, for example, which was only incorporated later on. Of course, these disparities are easily explained by the patchwork of local cultures and ethnicities. Still, the Roman empire during the 2nd century BC was far from territorially continuous, whereas in the middle of the 2nd century AD, it achieved its closest approximation of the empirical 'ideal-type'.

1 Iberia

The Iberian Peninsula, situated at the westernmost confines of the Mediterranean, saw the convergence of the two great urban and civic traditions of the East: Phoenician and Carthaginian on the one hand and Greek on the other. Their influence along the Mediterranean Iberian coastline and its confluence with the Atlantic Ocean is perceptible from the second half of the 1st millennium BC.

DOI: 10.4324/9781003450856-3

20 The Western Territories of Roman Expansion

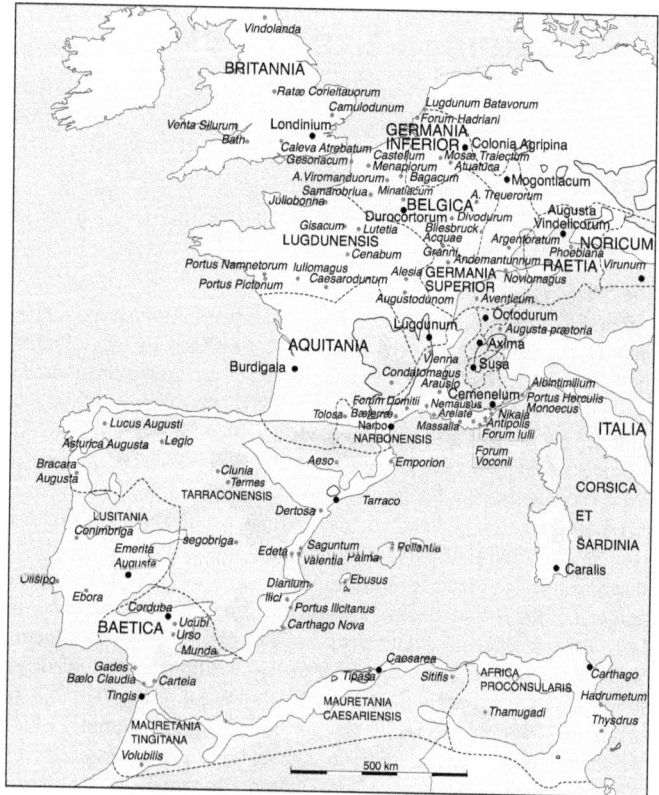

Figure 2.1 The Western Roman Empire, its provinces and provincial capitals. Cities mentioned in-text.

Source: Base map: Graticule. Infographics: © Vidal-Ros EOX.

Written records speak of the (probably mythical) foundation of Cádiz around the beginning of the 1st millennium BC by the Phoenicians of Tyre (although archaeological evidence suggests it may be later, around the 8th century BC). Around the same time as the foundation of *Massalia* (Marseille), roughly 600 BC, the Greeks of Phocaea founded *Emporion* (Ampurias) along the northeastern coast of Catalonia. Thus, the areas of influence of these two great political and urban traditions seem clear enough: Semitic to the south and southeast, extending to the isle and city of *Ebusus*, founded by the Phoenicians at the end of the 8th century or beginning of the 7th century BC; and Hellenistic to the northeast – constituting the westernmost portion of a vast territorial claim extending to modern-day Antibes and Nice, where Greek and Ligurian cultures met. The space between these two zones was attributable to one or the other at various times. Between Denia, the *Hemeroskopeion* (Latin *Dianium*), and Ampurias (*Emporion*) existed a large number of indigenous sites where Greek and Semitic influences can be found, although neither the Greeks nor the Phoenicians directly founded any of them. Research from the end of the 20th century, however, calls this otherwise clear-cut hypothesis into question. In the southeast of the Iberian Peninsula, for example, vestiges from *La Fonteta* (Guardamar del Segura) demonstrate the presence of Phoenician populations in interaction with local populations, while a mere 30 kilometres to the north, the architecture and organisation of La Picola (Santa Pola) betrays a Greek influence.

But this mélange of cultural influences wasn't limited to the coast. The Iberians mixed with all the peoples of the coast and the interior. The political and urban development of the Celtiberians in the valley of the Ebro, for example, was far from negligible. These social and urban organisations took root in embryonic but complex forms, and many would later offer fierce resistance to Roman conquerors. On the other hand, the familial social groups that populated the northern coast of Iberia, and their villages or *castros*, were less socially complex and closer in configuration to societies that developed between the Bronze Age and the arrival of Rome.

Florus (I, XXXIII, 5) tells us this ethnically and geographically discontinuous and fragmented panorama slowed Rome's expansion into the interior of the Iberian Peninsula but did not significantly impact the spatial organisation of Roman occupation. 2nd-century settlements in Iberia and the Balearic Islands (*Italica, Valentia, Palma,* and *Pollentia*) were not colonies of *civium romanorum* but more closely resembled military outposts. It would take Rome a century and a half to put in place a veritable territorial policy in the Iberian Peninsula, with only a handful of colonies founded and communities promoted by the middle of the 1st century BC.

The conflicts that came to exist between Romans on Hispanic soil were a delayed consequence of the Social War and shared the same root cause: the desire of the elites to obtain a citizenship previously denied them. Between the Sertorian War around 80 BC and the Battle

22 The Western Territories of Roman Expansion

Figure 2.2 Network of principal towns and main roads in *Hispania*.

Source: McCormick et al., 2013. GIS: L. Costa (CNRS – ArScAn). Base map: Graticule. Infographics: © Vidal-Ros EOX

of Munda in 45 BC, however, the population remained largely rural. Italy and Transalpine Gaul were only able to extricate themselves from this conflict by finally granting *ius Latii* or 'Latin Rights' to the local elites. As a result, the Italic population benefited from the foundation or promotion (to status of *municipium*, colony, etc.) of urban centres, while the veterans of the many demobilised legions were granted land. As demonstrated by an increase in urban activity, these evolutions signalled the dawning of a new age of prosperity for the colonies that resulted from this first phase of Roman conquests in Iberia until being disrupted once again, either by civil conflict or refoundation under Augustus (e.g., *Valentia*). Indeed, Augustus maintained an active policy of colonisation, subduing the northernmost territories at the end of the Cantabrian Wars in 19 BCE. It was during this period that the foundations of several outposts (*Asturica Augusta*, *Lucus Augusti*, and *Bracara Augusta*) were established, closely tied to the military presence tasked with subjugating this territory and controlling its gold resources. But the region's most important urban transformation occurred with the bestowal by Vespasian of *ius Latii* to all of Hispania around 73 or 74 AD. From this point on, the urban fabric increased in density in regions with existing urban infrastructure, like Baetica, and began expanding into the centre and the north of the peninsula. Here, the connection between civic integration and urbanisation is highly salient: certain *civitates* begin assimilating smaller settlements, such as *fora* and *vici*, dispersed across regions that until then were often devoid of any recognisable forms of urban life.

2 North Africa

Comprising a large coastline corresponding to modern-day Maghreb and parts of Libya, North Africa boasts a wide diversity of landscapes. From early on, Phoenician and then Carthaginian maritime traffic had a significant impact on the local Numidian populations.

For example, Carthage and the surrounding region, corresponding roughly to the borders of modern-day Tunisia, owes much to the expansion of the city of Tyre. Here, urbanisation was born of the interaction between Semitic colonisation and the Numidian world – a conjunction which, prior to the arrival of colonisers from the East, gave rise to civic infrastructures, an embryonic urban fabric, and the foundation of urban centres like Kerkouane (Tunisia), whose organisation is distinctly oriental. It also resulted in the foundation of a number of coastal cities and commercial *emporia*, connecting their hinterlands to the Mediterranean world.

Despite the famous expression '*Carthāgō dēlenda est*', the Punic city was never fully destroyed. The city and its territorial holdings were integrated into the empire's urban network. Rome used this network to augment commercial traffic between the coast and the free peoples of the Garamantes and the Fezzan residing in oases further inland. To the south, the great Roman territory *par excellence* of *Byzacium* (the modern-day Tunisian Sahel) benefited from Tyrian expansion and the urban infrastructure that accompanied it, connecting it to a rich agricultural hinterland and resulting in the development of such cities as *Hadrumetum* (Sousse) and *Thysdrus* (El Djem). A clear urban development also took place in valleys that interacted regularly with the interior (e.g., the Medjerda basin), while the steppes of the *Hautes Plaines* served as a home to nomadic peoples.

To the west lay the future territories of *Numidia* and *Mauretania*. These two large regions were less urbanised, except along the coast, which had long been a hotbed of maritime traffic coming from the eastern Mediterranean. Their interiors were controlled first by nomadic populations and later by the large relay cities that connected the coast to the inland. Further west still could be found *Mauretania Caesariensis* and *Mauretania Tingitana*. Here, various kingdoms maintained relations with the south of the Iberian Peninsula across the Alboran Sea and Roman Baetica, respectively. All together, these territories formed the cultural space known today as the 'Circle of the Strait'. The bordering areas, inhabited by local populations resistant to integration, were occupied by military camps built to control and oversee them, giving rise to hamlets and settlements of an agricultural nature and, as Roman territorialisation advanced, civic structures and urban sites.

Between the defeat of Carthage and 46 BC, no new settlements were founded in North Africa. In this vast area, as in the *Hispanias*, urban territorial policies only really appeared under Caesar and then Augustus and mainly concerned the northern coast of *Africa Proconsularis*. They were renewed under Tiberius and Trajan, who promoted a number of *civitates peregrinae* and port cities of Phoenician origin, resulting in a fairly loose urban fabric that became denser towards the coast and served to connect certain valleys to the interior.

3 Narbonensis and the Galliae

In the same way the Maghreb of eastern North Africa showed significantly greater urbanisation than the province's west, Roman Gaul exhibited earlier and more intense urbanisation in the south than the north. Here, Mediterranean influences were almost exclusively Greek once the Phocaeans founded Marseille and began mixing with the substantial existing Etruscan presence originating from the central Tyrrhenian Sea.

The Marseillais Phocaeans encountered a mosaic of local cultures (including Ibero-Languedocian and Celticised Ligurians), concentrated along the narrow strip of Mediterranean coastline where they settled and set up trading posts. Around this space, a deeply Hellenised culture developed through the diffusion of language, goods, and monetary standards, stimulating a social and economic dynamism that accelerated the appearance of sophisticated new social structures (for example, *civitates*-like political organisations appeared in great number) and settlements boasting Hellenic morphologies and architecture.

Further north, in *Gallia Comata*, a substantial network of urban centres known as *oppida* began to develop. Often fortified, these hilltop towns played an important economic and political role. Their rise to prominence coincided with the rise of the Aedui hegemony in 120 BC and an increasing level of organisation in the transalpine province. Despite the urban character of the *oppida*, their population density remained relatively low. And while generally organised around principal roadways, they lacked any kind of uniform urban grid – a kind of urbanism often referred to as a 'non-town' or 'low-density urbanism'. The space within the ramparts was shared by residential buildings and cultivated fields.

Rome's penetration into Gaul was accomplished through the intermediary of the Massiliote Greeks and their coastal trading posts, who called upon the Romans to help repel a series of recurring attacks that took place from the beginning of the 2nd century to 120 BC. Rome took this opportunity to further secure terrestrial and maritime passage for the Italic tradesmen established in Gaul since an unknown time, marking out the roadway that would later become known as the *Via Domitia*. This important highway bolstered traffic through the Alps and along the Rhodanian corridor to Spain. *Narbo Martius* (Narbonne) was the first colony under Roman law to be founded outside of Italy, along with two *fora* (marketplaces, absent Roman veterans or *deduction* settlers[1] and lacking a proper civic status): the *Forum Domitii* (near Montbazin, Hérault) and the *Forum Voconii* (in modern-day France's Var department). The Pompeian foundation of *Lugdunum Convenae* (Saint-Bertrand-de-Comminges), which controlled the upper valley of the Garonne and passage through the Pyrenees, was the last urban installation of this period. As with the regions discussed earlier, it was only from the time of the triumvirate that a true territorial policy of colonisation began – one that accelerated greatly from the second half of the 1st century, during Caesar's proconsulship and governance of transalpine Gaul.

In the 30s BC, Octavian and his right-hand man, Agrippa, inaugurated a new era of colonialism by establishing several colonies within the Rhone Valley and the new province of *Gallia Narbonensis*, including *Arausio* (Orange) and *Baeterrae* (Béziers). The *Forum Iulii* (Fréjus) was also promoted to the rank of colony at this time. In Belgian Gaul, a thin network of pre-Roman settlements gave rise to a network of administrative centres created *ex nihilo* between 27 and 13 BC, articulated around a road network built over the pre-existing routes that connected the Rhine to the English Channel. Subjugation of the local Alpine populations began from around 14 BC, and their

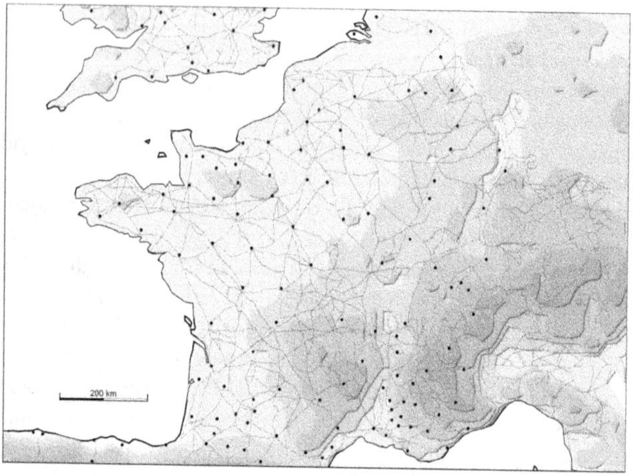

Figure 2.3 Network of principal towns and main roads in Gaul.

Source: McCormick et al., 2013. GIS: L. Costa (CNRS – ArScAn). Base map: Graticule. Infographics: © Vidal-Ros EOX.

defeat was definitively sealed with the Trophy of Augustus in Turbie (7 or 6 BC). Henceforth, communications between Italy and Gaul became more direct, thanks in large part to the construction of the *Via Iulia Augusta* (13 and 12 BC) and the existence of a series of small Alpine cities guaranteeing its safety. This network was further completed under the Julio-Claudian dynasty, with Latin Rights granted to the Three Gauls, probably between Claudius and Domitian. Under the Flavian and Antonine dynasties, the number of colonies was very small, with only limited promotions of certain *civitates peregrinae* to the rank of honorary colonies. In any case, by the time the imperial territorial organisation of Roman Gaul was mostly complete, the locations of most Roman cities corresponded fairly well to those of the ancient *oppida*, without reproducing them exactly.

4 The Germanies and Britain

Having been integrated somewhat later into the empire, these two territories are similar in several ways. Most notably, they were highly militarised due to the presence of unconquered neighbouring populations.

The two Germanies were originally military districts, excised from the first Belgian Gaul of the Augustan era and defended by a series of military installations along the Rhine River, reinforced following the Varian Disaster and Rome's failed occupation of the east bank.

It was probably only under Trajan that Latin law was applied to *Germania*. Organised territorially by its two large rivers, the Rhine and the Danube, the region boasted a diversity of cultures, concentrated in larger urban centres, similar to large *oppida*, and smaller, simpler hamlets. North of the line that would later become the route linking the Rhine from *Colonia Agrippinensis* (Cologne) to *Gesoriacum* (Boulogne) at the North Sea, these *oppidum*-like structures were scarcer. While never fully depopulated, this relatively weak urban geography remained characteristic of the region throughout Roman rule (with the exception of the *Frisiavones* and *Cananefates*, who were organised into proper *civitates*). A dispersed style of habitat dominated the mouths of the Scheldt, the Meuse, and the Rhine, consisting of farms (N. Roymans' 'non-villa landscapes') and smaller military and trade settlements set behind the coastal dunes. In this case, as in the northwestern Iberian Peninsula, urbanisation was not as significantly linked to civic organisation. A single important roadway ran along the Rhine from Cologne to the North Sea and *Lugdunum Batavorum* (near Leiden, in the Netherlands). Two colonies and three *municipia*, closely connected to these two terrestrial and fluvial axes, form the entirety of the region's sparse urban network.

Roman Brittany was conquered by Emperor Claudius less than a century after Caesar's expedition, which itself was without territorial consequence. The grouped settlements that could be found there were limited to the areas closest to the mainland and only appeared during the first century BC. They were a direct result of intensified trade with Belgian Gaul and gave rise to state organisations governed by kinglets, as attested by the money they minted in their own name or that of their people. Such settlements were concentrated around a central place at some important crossroads or passageway. Caesar described what the Bretons called an *oppidum* as a place protected by simple natural defences (*Bellum Gallicum*, V, 21). These were probably *enclosed oppida*, not to be confused with the *territorial oppida* mentioned in anglophone historical literature, which were rather sparse and dispersed habitats of just a few hectares. These political and territorial structures enabled the production of consumer goods destined for the commercial circuits of northern Gaul.

28 *The Western Territories of Roman Expansion*

Figure 2.4 Network of principal towns and main roads in *Britannia*.

Source: McCormick et al., 2013. GIS: L. Costa (CNRS – ArScAn). Base map: Graticule. Infographics: © Vidal-Ros EOX.

Roman occupation of these territories thus progressed from the southeast to the north and west. First military camps were established, where troops charged with surveillance of the region were housed. Then came the colonies themselves: *Camulodunum* (Colchester), capital of the province until the foundation of *Londinium*

(London). Other urban centres cropped up in close proximity to the former administrative centres of indigenous populations. The army, advancing north and west, also came to occupy new territory, always according to the same process of civic integration. In the region's northernmost confines, military outposts eventually grew into important towns following Rome's departure from the island. Despite the fact that the population remained largely rural, each community, politically organised into a *civitas*, boasted its own capital and urban architectural landscape. These principal cities co-existed with small towns, urban in appearance but unplanned and devoid of any civic function, albeit deeply integrated into the new economic system. They emerged as *vici* at strategic crossroads or in the shadow of military camps.

Note

1 Deduction was the process of relocating a group of Roman citizens from their civitas of origin to some other one. Such citizens were 'deducted' (*deducere*) from the census of the first civitas and inscribed in that of the second, as it was impossible to be a citizen of two civitates at the same time.

Bibliography

Abascal, J. M., Espinosa, U., *La Ciudad hispano-romana. Privilegio y poder*, Logroño, Colegio Oficial de Arquitectos, 1989.

Aounallah, S., *Pagus, castellum et civitas. Études d'épigraphie et d'histoire sur le village et la cité en Afrique romaine*, Pessac, Ausonius Éditions, 2010.

Badie, A., Gailledrat, E., Moret, P., Rouillard, P., Sánchez, M. J., Sillières, P., *Le site antique de La Picola à Santa Pola (Alicante, Espagne)*, Paris – Madrid, Casa de Velázquez, 2000.

Bedon, R., *Les villes des trois Gaules de César à Néron dans le contexte historique territorial et politique*, Paris, Picard, 1999.

Dondin-Payre, M., Loriot, X., Ou une communauté était organisée en cité, ou elle n'existait pas: L'administration interne de la Bretagne, in *Rome et l'Occident: Gouverner l'Empire (IIe siècle av. J.-C. – IIe siècle ap. J.-C.)*, Rennes, Presses Universitaires de Rennes, 2009, pp. 413–420.

Fentress, E., Coercive Urbanism: The Roman Impact on North African Towns, in O. Belvedere, J. Bergemann (eds.), *Imperium Romanum: Romanization between Colonization and Globalization*, Palermo, Università di Palermo, 2021, pp. 165–178.

Gorges, J. G. (ed.), *Les villes de la Lusitanie romaine. Hiérarchies et territoires*, Paris, Editions du CNRS, 1990.

Hanoune, R. (dir.), *Les villes romaines du Nord de la Gaule. Vingt ans de recherches nouvelles, Actes du XXVe colloque international de HALMA-IPEL UMR CNRS 8164*, Lille, Revue du Nord Hors-série, 2007.

Helas, S., Marzoli, D. (eds.), *Phönizisches und punisches Städtewesen. Akten der internationalen Tagung in Rom vom 21. bis 23. Februar 2007, Rome, 2007*, Mayence, Von Zabern, 2009.

Lafon, X., Marc, J. Y., Sartre, M., *La ville antique*, in J. L. Pinol (dirs.), *Histoire de l'Europe urbaine*, Paris, Éditions du Seuil, 2011 [Reedition].

Laurence, R., Cleary, S. E., Sears, G., *The City in The Roman West c. 250 BC – c. AD 250*, Cambridge, Cambridge University Press, 2011.

Leveau, P., Rémy, B. (dirs.), *La ville des Alpes occidentales à l'époque romaine: Actes du colloque international "La ville des Alpes occidentales à l'époque romaine", qui s'est tenue* [sic] *les 6, 7 et 8 octobre 2006 à Grenoble à l'Université Pierre Mendès France, UFR Sciences Humaines*, Grenoble, CRHIPA, 2008.

López de Castro, J. L. (ed.), *Las ciudades fenicio-púnicas en el Mediterráneo Occidental*, Almería, Universidad de Almería, 2007.

Mahjoubi, A., *Villes et structures urbaines de la province romaine d'Afrique*, Tunis, Centre de Publication Universitaire, 2000.

Mangas Manjarrés, J., *Leyes coloniales y municipales de la Hispania romana*, Madrid, Arco Libros, 2001.

Mann, J. C., The Cities of the Roman Empire, in J.-C. Mann, Britain and the Roman Empire, Variorum, Aldershot, 1996, pp. 101–122 = Les cités sous l'Empire romain, in F. Hurlet, *Rome et l'Occident: Gouverner l'Empire (IIe siècle av. J.-C. – IIe siècle ap. J.-C.)*, Rennes, Presses Universitaires de Rennes, 2009, pp. 387–311.

Mateos, P., Olcina Doménech, M. H., Pizzo, A., Schattner, T. G., (coords.), *Small Towns, una realidad urbana en la Hispania romana*, (2 vols.), Merida, Instituto de Arqueología de Mérida, 2022.

McCormick, M., *et al.*, Roman Road Network (Version 2008), in *DARMC Scholarly Data Series*, Cambridge, Center for Geographic Analysis, Harvard University, 2013 [Online: https://doi.org/10.7910/DVN/TI0KAU].

Nogales Basarrate, T. (ed.), *Ciudades Romanas de Hispania*, Roma, "L'Erma" di Bretschneider, 2021.

Nogales Basarrate, T. (ed.), *Ciudades Romanas de Hispania II. Cities of Roman Hispania II*, Roma, "L'Erma" di Bretschneider, 2022.

Ortiz-de-Urbina, E. (coord.), *Ciudadanías, Ciudades y Comunidades cívicas en Hispania (de los Flavios a los Severos)*, Sevilla, Universidad de Sevilla, 2019.

Reddé, M., Van Andringa, W. (dirs.), *La naissance des capitales de cités en Gaule Chevelue*, Paris, Gallia, 2015, pp. 72–81.

Wacher, J., *The Towns of Roman Britain*, London, Book Club Associates, 1974.

Zanker, P., *La città romana*, Roma – Bari, Laterza, 2013.

3 The Colonial Myth

1 Choosing a Location

In Book I, Chapter IV of *De architectura*, Vitruvius provides a list of criteria for choosing the location for a new city. Some of these are Hippocratic in nature: humidity, temperature, weather, and distance from swamps were all spatial qualities the Romans considered necessary for harmony, inasmuch as they parallel certain qualities of the human body. In the beginning of Chapter 3, however, which deals with the construction of ramparts and towers, Vitruvius – directly addressing the hypothetical founder of a new city, in a rather unexpected fashion – evokes a whole series of important material factors: workable land, roadways, waterways, and (access to) a port.

In accordance with the socio-political landscape of his time, Vitruvius sees the ideal Roman city as autarkic, or at least autonomous. But what were actual settlements like in their physical environments? R. Bedon has explored a variety of factors that were taken into consideration during the foundation of cities in the Three Gauls and which were valid for many other cities in the Roman West. Among the physical criteria, access to water (rivers, lakes, etc.) was critical, not only for hydration (which is satisfied easily enough by digging wells, as in many *domus*), but also for the evacuation of waste and, of course, the transportation of persons and goods, principally by river (Vitruvius, *De architectura*, Chapter 4). This is why in Gaul, more so than in any other region of the empire (with the possible exception of the Danube River basin), Strabo describes the interaction of roadways and navigable rivers as the 'work of Providence', the Greek *pronoia*: the promise of an environment ripe for exploitation. The work of P. Moret has made it possible to establish that the main cities and strongholds (*metropoleis, emporia*, and *phrouria*) were located precisely at these points of interaction, like so many bridgeheads lending structure to the network. Lyon, capital and quintessential *emporion*, stands at the confluence of the Rhône and the Saône, two primary waterways, each connected to various other rivers leading to the North Sea and the English Channel. Through Narbonne, Toulouse is connected to the Mediterranean via the River Aude (after a short passage over land) and, through Bordeaux, to the ocean by way of the Garonne. Indeed, it was in these major urban nodes, and at the interface between the sea and river routes, that guilds of *nautae* or 'boatmen' were first established. They operated in an extraterritorial fashion, by virtue of the fact that their work depended on the course of a river. There were thus *nautae* of the Durance, of the Rhône and the Saone, of the *Lemanus*, and also of specific populations, such as the *Parisii*.

The arrangement of rivers and roads was particularly decisive in the urban hierarchy of regions that were conquered later. The organisation of main roadways helped determine the foundation and development of larger cities atop the urban hierarchy: Amiens (*Samarobriva*); Trier (*Augusta Treverorum*), where the road splits westward toward the English Channel and eastward to the Rhine; and Bavay (*Bagacum*) and Tongeren (*Atuatuca*), between the Roman fleet port of Boulogne (*Gesoriacum*) and Cologne (*Colonia Agrippinensis*) on the Rhine.

On the Atlantic coast, estuaries played a fundamental role. Access inland, to the 'navigable plains' of which Strabo spoke, depended largely on rivers and the tide. At *Olisipo* (Lisbon), Strabo tells us (*Geographica*, III.3.1) that the Tagus estuary permitted the passage of ships carrying up to 10,000 *amphorae*. The Loire estuary no doubt played the same role: on both banks of the river and at its mouth, the *Portus Pictonum* or *Ratiatum* (Rezé) and the *Portus Namnetorum* or *Condeuincum* (Nantes) each served a different *civitas*. The archaeological excavations carried out in these two cities have made it possible to identify various elements characteristic of ports: monumentalised wooden and dry-stone quays, warehouses, and baths dotted the shores of the Loire.

Social and religious components played an important role as well. In founding cities, Rome increased the density of pre-existing urban grids and created others where they had once been absent. Distance played a fundamental role, and principal urban centres were sometimes relocated to the vicinity of former *oppida*, which then disappeared or merged with the new urban entity. This was the case of *Andemantunnum* (Langres), which retains the location and name of the former *oppidum* of the *Lingons* (proof that hilltop towns were not always razed or depopulated). The same is true of *Cemenelum* (the neighbourhood of Cimiez in Nice, France), founded to serve as the region's administrative centre and provincial capital at the foot of the *oppidum* of the *Vedianti*, just three kilometres from the Greek trading post of Nikaïa (Nice). At the opposite end of the spectrum, inhabitants of the *oppida* of Titelberg (Luxembourg), Kasselt, and Martberg were moved 20–70 kilometres to the newly founded city of *Augusta Treverorum* (Trier, Germany), situated at a bend in the River Moselle and along the main roadways leading to the Rhine. Finally, during the Augustan era, the *Tungri* city of *Atuatuca* (Tongeren, Belgium) served as a new home to rural populations that had survived the Gallic War. Prior to its foundation *ex nihilo*, they had no well-identified political centre.

2 Naming and Renaming

Myths bear witness to the way a society, from one century to the next, perceives the world. In this respect, Roman society was confronted with a difficulty: how to articulate its vision of the city-state with respect to the territory around it; and then, as it expanded, with the rest of the Italian peninsula; and finally, in relation to the whole of the conquered Mediterranean world and especially those regions where urban life already existed. Furthermore, how were the hierarchies and social structures of newly incorporated peoples and spaces, in all their diversity, to be integrated? To give some semblance of spatial and chronological continuity to this heterogenous group of territories, cities, and towns, it was necessary to name or rename them. Several solutions presented themselves.

The names of local populations in *civitates*, provinces, and towns sometimes remained unchanged following the Romans' arrival (although, as we've seen, they were often relocated and consolidated to form new *civitates*). As provincial borders migrated (which became less frequent as time went on), Rome could choose to take into account old territorial and administrative organisations or transform them completely. But the names were often conserved.

However, this process did not reflect any one overriding strategy or policy of territorial development that might have been applied in a top-down fashion to local populations. Rather, it resulted from the interplay of actors at multiple levels, starting with local representatives of the distant Roman power. The local elites, each with their own particular ambitions, and all those who survived the war and remained after defeat, also played a role. In modifying existing spatial organisations or creating new hybrid ones, they became carriers of a new 'system of meaning'. In this way, the final shape of the whole territory, beyond the city itself, was not the result of a single, unilateral will or action. Take, for example, the case of *Belgium*. For Caesar, during the time of the Gallic War, this was a small region in Northern Gaul, situated between the Seine, the Marne, and the Rhine. For Strabo, *Belgium* extended from the Loire to the Rhine. For Pliny, these same rivers delimited the space attributed to peoples such as the Helvetii (whose territory actually extended well beyond them). It was not until the end of the first century AD and the separation of the two military districts of the *Germaniae* that the limits of Belgian Gaul became stable and took the form they would retain until the end of the 3rd century.

These examples allow us to measure the extent to which, in a little more than a century, Roman colonialism was subject to various disruptions and necessarily took into account multiple spatial realities. Local place names, geopolitical tensions, common origins, and geographical traditions, imprinted upon by the Roman administration, all gave rise to a complex spatiality with, as P. Le Roux has well demonstrated, an equally complex urban toponymy.

Just as with modern and contemporary settlers who named cities, states, and regions in their own language and in honour of their sovereign rulers (e.g., Queenstown, Georgetown, Carolina, Louisiana), in reference to native tribes (e.g., Alabama, Kansas), and sometimes with composite forms (e.g., Fort Apache; Iowa City), the same logic was applied to ancient cities and towns. Thus, as demonstrated by R. Bedon, the majority (70%) of cities in Gaul bore names of indigenous inspiration (e.g., *Andemantunnum*, modern-day Langres; and *Cenabum*, modern-day Orléans). Cities with Latin names represent only 13% (e.g., *Colonia Agrippinensis*, modern-day Cologne), while 15% of cities had a hybrid name (e.g., *Caesarodunum*, modern-day Tours; *Iuliomagus*, modern-day Angers; *Augustodunum*, modern-day Autun; and *Castellum Menapiorum*, modern-day Cassel).

Toponymy was thus a means of appropriating a space while at the same time allowing for spatial continuity over long distances, with the use of Latin tying new regions to the rest of the empire and the Latin world. Where local names were preserved, and especially when Romans chose to maintain the existing urban hierarchy, this continuity comprised a temporal component as well. Finally, naming conventions sometimes accompanied the transition between the old world and the new, as when an original toponym was preserved or an ethnonym was added to a new name, even if the city in question was founded *ex nihilo* and at considerable distance from the urban centre that originally bore the name (e.g., *Augusta Viromanduorum*, modern-day Saint-Quentin, and *Augusta Nemausus*, today's Nîmes).

3 The Appropriation of Physical Environments

Previously, we examined the territorial transformations brought about by the legal codifications of the *agrimensores*. Now, we will look at how the physical environment itself evolved as a result of colonialism and agricultural exploitation.

As we have seen, the foundation of Roman settler colonies was primarily a consequence of overpopulation and the need to allocate land to demobilised soldiers. However, once the land had been assigned and distributed, territories still had to be developed and organised, the land worked, and taxes collected. Centuriation not only led to the establishment of a cadastral tax base, but it also served as a preliminary manner of organising the city spatially – a kind of topographical instrument employed in the management of property, land, and wetlands. The knowledge and techniques of lawyers, engineers, surveyors, and agronomists were invaluable in the shaping of colonial landscapes designed to produce more and foster trade.

A primary concern was the transportation of water. Engineering projects such as aqueducts brought water to some high point in the city, from where it could be redirected with sufficient pressure to provision thermal baths and the second floors of certain homes. In Nîmes, for example, human consumption alone could not account for the construction of a 45-kilometre aqueduct, given what other sources of water were already available to the city. In fact, the abutment of the Nîmes aqueduct divides in two at the coastline, giving rise to an outlet canal responsible for discharging excess water from the former lake of Clausonne into the Gardon River – thus connecting different watersheds and allowing for the development of newly conquered lands. Likewise, the draining of the Fucine Lake in Italy, undertaken at the time of Emperor Claudius, was done in order to make use of the fertile soil under the water. P. Leveau has shown how the operation was financed by ceding the recovered land to wealthy investors.

Another example, examined by the same author, comes from the aqueducts of Arles, which conveyed water not to a city centre but to the Arlesian countryside; specifically, the watermill complex of Barbegal, which operated between the 2nd and 3rd centuries AD. The water from the aqueducts was used to drive the mill's 16 millstones, capable of producing up to 4.5 tons of flour per day – enough for the individual daily consumption (350 grams) of roughly 12,500 individuals. That is, the entire colony of Arles. Both municipal and private initiatives existed, as demonstrated by the Pont d'Aël. This aqueduct near Aoste, Italy was built in 3 BC by one *C. Avillius Caimus*, and the central arch bears the word '*privatum*'. The water it carried was used for sawing the local marble, known as *Bardiglio*. Even though the aqueduct was privately owned, an investment of this nature could only have been undertaken within the context of the construction of the nearby town of *Augusta Praetoria*.

Less obvious in the archaeological record are interventions undertaken to transform wetlands, although they resulted in a profoundly altered landscape. The need to develop these lands stemmed from the physical constraints of the Italic and Mediterranean regions. The steep topography delimiting the narrow coastal plains resulted in fertile marshy areas, which could be converted into workable land – but only after being cleared and developed.

The draining of lagoons, by means of outlets that diverted excess water to the sea, transformed thousands of hectares of marshland for the purposes of agricultural exploitation. The work of paleoenvironmental and archaeogeographic researchers has revealed evidence of such interventions throughout the Languedoc region between the Alps and the Pyrenees.

As previously mentioned, centuriation was the most widely used method of distributing, planning, and organising the *ager publicus* and the newly incorporated land. The study of aerial photographs as well as archaeological excavations near the ancient colony of Orange, in the Rhone Valley, have brought to light a series of irrigation canals, as well as a whole system of ditches delimiting various plots of land, designed to evacuate water from the flood plains. In the specific case of this region, it is even possible to determine where agricultural divisions were located, thanks to the discovery in the 1950s of *formae* ('maps') inscribed on marble and giving an account of three major surveying operations. The physical appropriation of land was thus accompanied by its functional appropriation, made visible in this case by

38 *The Colonial Myth*

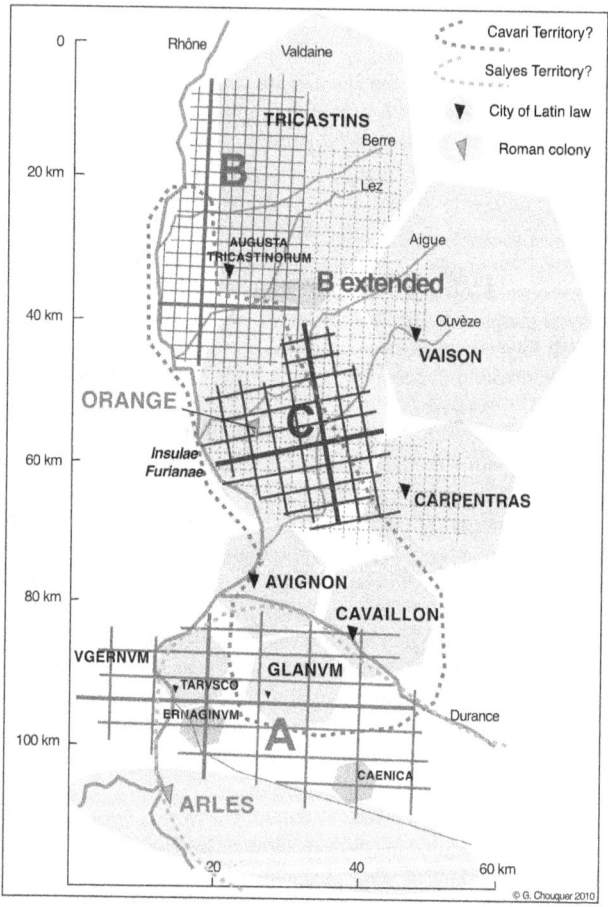

Figure 3.1 Centuriations of *Arausio* (Orange).
Source: (© Chouquer and Favory, 2001).

a geographical and cadastral representation displayed at the colony's *forum*. Among the various possible interpretations, this document details the way in which the country was divided and the status and fiscal systems of the lands in question – not only those whose direction fell to the colony of *Arausio* (Orange), but also those of nearby cities.

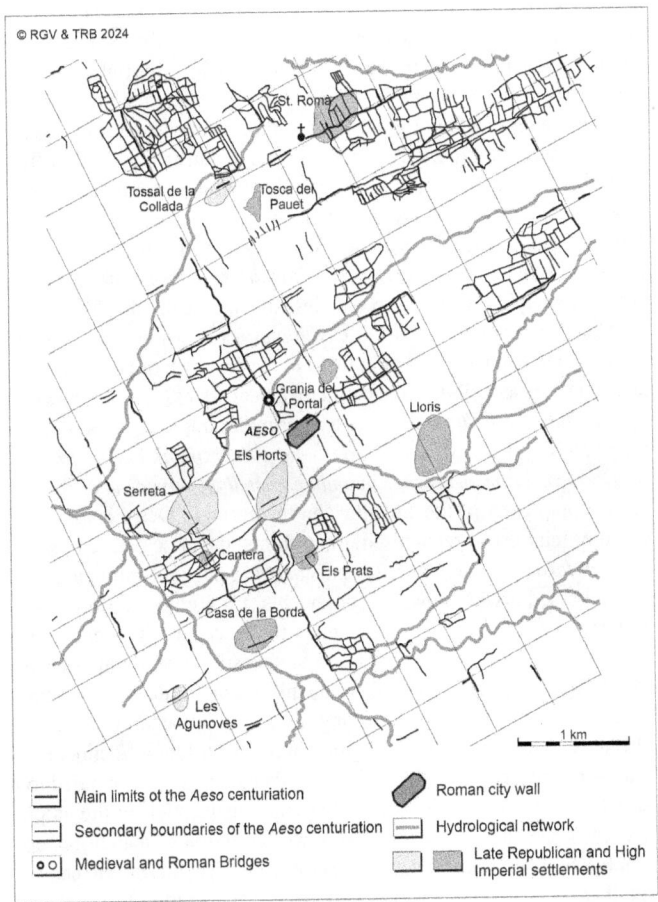

Figure 3.2 Centuriation of the territory around the city *Aeso* (Isona, Spain), in divisions of 15 × 15 *actus*, with distribution of rural agricultural settlements.

Source: Reyes Bellmunt, González Villaescusa, García Biosca, 2000. Infographics: © Vidal-Ros EOX.

4 Urban Discontinuity and Civic Continuity

Paradoxical as it may seem, the title of this section reflects the ambiguity of urban forms created by Rome. The diverse forms of grouped habitats encountered by the Romans during their territorial expansion contributed to a certain toponymic ambiguity, as did the many divergences inherent in the original Roman model, translated into diverse legal expressions exported from Rome and in constant evolution. Territoriality was thus a kind of cooperative evolution: from allied kingdoms to provinces and prefectures, a wide range of spatial realities coexisted. In the early days of the Empire, these were classified according to various legal categories (*fora, conciliabula, coloniae*, etc.), but with time they merged and became less toponymically diverse.

The *Lex (Rubria) de Gallia Cisalpina*, set down between 49 and 42 BC, when Roman law was granted to the province of northern Italy, lays out the responsibilities of municipal magistrates (*duoviri* and *quattuorviri iure dicundo*) and serves as a prime example of urban discontinuity. The variety of urban forms – *oppidum, municipium, colonia, praefectura, forum, vicus, conciliabulum, castellum, territorium* – testifies to the complexity of the situation 'on the ground'. Despite appearing on an official list of recognised urban forms, the civic nature of *praefectura, fora, vici, conciliabula*, and *castella* remained ambiguous and encompassed a wide range of settlements, from cities and urban settlements (*oppida, municipia, coloniae*) to dispersed settlements in the form of farms and *villae*. In addition to its institutional definition (that of a region's capital), and to illustrate this notion of 'urban discontinuity', it's worth noting that, according to M. Tarpin, the term '*vicus*' was also used to refer to an isolated group of urban buildings, distinct from the capital and connected by roads. Of course, this corresponded to a variety of spatial realities, depending on their location in the empire and when they are first mentioned in written sources. In addition, epigraphic sources make no mention of *vici* on the Mediterranean coast of the Iberian Peninsula, whereas they occur frequently in Gaul. Nor do they mention territorial *fora* in North Africa. Among English-speaking historians, urban settlements that are not mentioned explicitly as *vici* in written or epigraphic sources are given the more neutral appellation of 'small towns'.

The modern mind, born in a world of nation-states, struggles to apprehend the territorial discontinuity created by these geographic enclaves, not to mention the extraterritorial configurations suggested by the texts of the *gromatici veteres*. To get beyond the idea of a 'compact city' and better understand the complexities of ancient times, the concept of 'discontinuous urbanisation' is worth borrowing from geographers and urbanists.

Keeping this and the work of P. Le Roux and M. Tarpin in mind, let's return to the various urban categories mentioned earlier. *Oppidum* is a global concept and refers to the political centre of a territory: the capital of a *civitas*. This was true regardless of its status (Roman or Latin colony, municipality, city under Latin Law, or city of *peregrini*), which, at this stage, was of little or no importance to the Roman administration. Urban structures could already be identified thanks to the progressive monumentalisation of urban functions. Other settlements could also be found within the territory of the capital, but necessarily lacked its civic functions. Such was the case of *vici* – a term also used to refer to a city street or neighbourhood that boasted its own distinct spatiality, albeit within a *civitas* and thus a single territorial configuration. The inhabitants of such geographically distinct districts were no less citizens of the capital than those of its contiguous districts. The same was true for other districts that were topologically discontinuous: the inhabitants of any districts beyond the walls of the capital were still considered its citizens. Likewise for *fora*. Territorial *fora* (as opposed to the *forum* in the centre of a city) were marketplaces associated with a capital – a kind of administrative district that enjoyed a certain level of autonomy, thanks to a legal status very close to that of a *municipium* but lacking an *ius dicere*. In the early stages of Rome's transition from city-state to empire, this 'quasi-civic' structure, with its dispersed settlements, made it the ideal spatial formula, especially in the West, for producing a topological continuum without having to resort to the heavy investments required for the foundation of a whole colony. This helps explain the frequent promotion of *fora* (as compared to *vici* or *castella*), as the inhabitants of such territorial organisations would eventually be made to form a *civitas*, equipped with its own territory.

Finally, the term *conciliabulum* referred both to an administrative unit and a meeting place for Roman citizens, associated with a Roman colony or placed under the direct authority of Rome. With the municipalisation of 89 BC, *conciliabula* became *municipia* – a common outcome for the various spatial solutions employed by Rome.

None of these categories, however, implied any kind of lesser or 'sub-civic' status. Remember: the basic Roman unit was the *civitas*;

free men were citizens of their place of residence, a key element of the *census*, that most essential of tax registers. If a single building housed the *curia*, it was necessarily located in the primary urban centre – but the inhabitants of secondary settlements played a civic role no different from residents of the capital. To reach the capital of any territory, one left one's home and crossed a discontinuous architectural landscape without ever leaving the capital's territory, the *civitas*. Topographical discontinuity did not imply social discontinuity.

P. Arnaud, furthermore, has thoroughly explained the meaning of toponyms that refer to settlements separated from the city by physical discontinuities – parts of the city which were urban in appearance but whose land was characterised as rural. Such was the case of the *suburbia*: inhabited suburbs outside the ramparts, detached from the *continentia*, but connected nonetheless to the city.

Bibliography

Arnaud, P., Vers une définition géodynamique des suburbia: Eléments pour une zonation des zones péri-urbaines, in R. Bedon (ed.), *Suburbia. Les faubourgs en Gaule romaine et dans les régions voisines, Caesarodunum*, Limoges, Presses universitaires de Limoges, 22, 1998, pp. 63–81.

Arnaud, P., La gestion des ressources naturelles et l'intégration économique des provinces d'Occident dans le processus de développement et de romanisation d'après Strabon: Topique littéraire et document historique, in *Espaces intégrés et ressources naturelles dans l'Empire romain. Actes du colloque de l'Université de Laval – Québec (5–8 mars 2003)*, Besançon, Institut des Sciences et Techniques de l'Antiquité, 2004, pp. 25–38.

Béal, J. C., Les "nautes armés" de Lutèce: Mythe ou réalité? *Revue archéologique*, 40–42, 2005, pp. 315–337.

Bedon, R. (ed.), Suburbia. Les faubourgs en Gaule romaine et dans les régions voisines, Tours, *Caesarodonum*, 22, 1998.

Cavallaro, A. M., Il "Pondel": Un acquedotto privato ai margini della "Via delle Gallie", in C. Belardelli, L. De Maria (eds.), *Le vie romane nel Lazio e nel Mediterraneo, Atti delle giornate di studio (Roma, 28 maggio 2001)*, Roma, Palombi, 2002, pp. 105–114.

Chouquer, G., Favory, F., *L'arpentage romain. Histoire des textes, droit, techniques*, Paris, Errance, 2001.

Compatangelo-Soussignan, R., Le littoral atlantique de la péninsule Ibérique antique et l'*anachysis* de Poseidonion d'Apamée, in E. Hermon, A. Watelet (dirs.), *La gestion intégrée des bords de l'eau,*

Proceedings of the Sudbury Workshop, April 12–14, 2012, Actes de l'atelier Savoirs et pratiques de gestion intégrée des bords de l'eau – Riparia, Sudbury, 12–14 avril 2012, Oxford, BAR International Series, 2014, pp. 179–185.

Fabre, G., Fiches, J. L., Paillet, J. L. (dirs.), *L'aqueduc de Nîmes et le pont du Gard: Archéologie, géosystème, histoire*, 2nd edition, Paris, CNRS Éditions, 2000.

González Villaescusa, R., Reims capitale de la Gaule Belgique et le réseau des villes de la province. Un essai, in R. González Villaescusa, J. Ruiz de Arbulo (eds.), *Simulacra Romae II*, Reims, Bulletin de la Société archéologique champenoise, Mémoire n° 19, 2010, pp. 201–206.

González Villaescusa, R., La construction de la *Gallia Belgica* de l'Antiquité à nos jours à travers les auteurs anciens et l'historiographie moderne, in P. Cattelain, I. Incoul, E. Warmenbol (dirs.), *Fortissimi sunt Belgae*, Treignes, Editions du Cedarc, 2023, pp. 35–44.

González Villaescusa, R., Jacquemin, T., *Gallia Belgica*: Un objet sans revendication nationale, *Études Rurales*, 188, 2011, pp. 93–111 = *Gallia Belgica*: An Entity with No National Claim, *Etudes rurales*, 188, 2011 [Online: https://doi.org/10.4000/etudesrurales.9499].

Le Roux, P., *Vicus* et *castellum* en Lusitanie sous l'Empire, in Actas del Coloquio Les campagnes de Lusitanie romaine: Occupation du sol et habitat), *Studia Historica. Historia antigua*, 10–11, 1992–1993 [1994], pp. 151–160.

Le Roux, P., Géographie péninsulaire et épigraphie romaine, in G. Cruz Andreotti, P. Le Roux, P. Moret (eds.), *La invención de una geografía de la Península Ibérica. II. La época imperial (Actas del coloquio Internacional celebrado en la Casa de Velázquez de Madrid entre el 3 y el 4 de marzo de 2005)*, Madrid – Málaga, Casa de Velázquez – Diputación de Málaga, 2007a, pp. 197–219.

Le Roux, P., L'invention de la province romaine d'Espagne citérieure de 197 a. C. à Agrippa, in G. Cruz Andreotti, P. Le Roux, P. Moret (eds.), *La invención de una geografía de la Península Ibérica. I. La época republicana (Actas del coloquio Internacional celebrado en la Casa de Velázquez de Madrid entre el 3 y el 4 de marzo de 2005)*, Madrid – Málaga, casa de Velázquez – Diputación de Málaga, 2007b, pp. 117–134.

Leveau, P., Mentalité économique et grands travaux hydrauliques: Le drainage du lac Fucin aux origines d'un modèle, *Annales. Economies, sociétés, civilisations*, 48e année, 1, 1993, pp. 3–16.

Leveau, P., Les moulins de Barbegal 1986–2006, in J. P. Brun, J. L. Fiches (dirs.), *Énergie hydraulique et machines élévatrices d'eau dans l'Antiquité*, Naples, Publications du Centre Jean Bérard, 2007, pp. 185–189.

Moret, P., Strabon et les fleuves gaulois, in F. Olmer, R. Roure (dirs.), *Les Gaulois au fil de l'eau. Actes du 37e colloque de l'Association française pour l'étude de l'âge du fer (Montpellier, 8–11 mai 2013)*, Bordeaux, Ausonius Éditions, 2015, pp. 217–234.

Mouchard, J., Guitton, D. (eds.), *Les ports romains dans les Trois Gaules. Entre Atlantique et eaux intérieures*, Paris, Gallia, 2020.

Reyes Bellmunt, T., González Villaescusa, R., Garcia Biosca, J. E., Estudio del ager aesonensis (Isona y Conca Dellà, Pallars Jussà), *Arqueología y Territorio Medieval*, 8, 2000, pp. 125–160.

Ruoff Väänänen, E., *Studies on the Italian Fora*, Wiesbaden, F. Steiner, 1978.

Sánchez-Moreno Ellart, C., *Lex Rubria de Gallia Cisalpina*, in R. S. Bagnall, K. Brodersen, C. B. Champion, A. Erskine, S. R. Huebner (eds.), *The Encyclopedia of Ancient History*, Malden – Oxford – Chichester, Wiley-Blackwell, 2013, pp. 4045–4047.

Tarpin, M., *Vici et pagi dans l'Occident romain*, Roma, École Française de Rome, 2002.

4 The Empire's Urban Relays

1 Centrality

To control and exert cultural influence across its newly conquered territories, the Roman empire leveraged a network of central places – capitals or '*chefs-lieux*' – where inhabitants shared a common urban lifestyle.

At first, centrality was a direct consequence of the multiple functions fulfilled by individual cities, which both reinforced the urban hierarchy and led to greater (and grander) architectural monumentalisation. Terrestrial, fluvial, and maritime routes connected these various nodes, while easily converted coinage and a universal (or easily transposable) system of weights and measurements facilitated the flow of goods and foodstuffs from the various peripheral regions of the empire to central places, including Rome. Pliny the Younger (*Panegyric in Praise of Trajan*, XXXIX) and Aelius Aristides (*Regarding Rome*, 11–12) highlight this process of centralisation, the latter describing the empire's territory as the sum of individual territories of the *civitates* that comprised it.

The urban gigantism and macrocephaly characteristic of a relatively small number of cities in the empire has been linked to the low level of urbanism present there prior to Romanisation. Indeed, this lack of urbanisation may have engendered a kind of urban 'hyper-development'. This was certainly the case with *Bagacum* (Bavay), whose public centre or *forum* occupied 2.5 hectares or 2.5% of the city's total surface area (approximately 100 hectares) in the first century AD. The large Roman cities that appeared in regions with a more recent and looser urban fabric very quickly accumulated more functions and grew in population. Their distribution appears to have been relatively sparse, with each city responsible for a very large territory. Organising such vast spaces

46 *The Empire's Urban Relays*

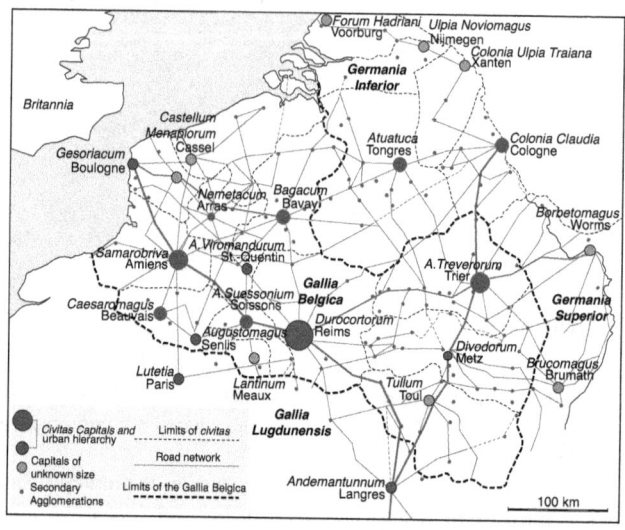

Figure 4.1 Network of principal towns in Belgian Gaul, superimposed on the province's *civitates*, showing the hierarchy of primary and secondary settlements.

Source: González-Villaescusa, 2010; Guillerat et al., 2020. Base map: Graticule. Infographics: © Vidal-Ros EOX.

required the intervention and cooperation of other, smaller urban centres. The average distance between cities in the north of Gaul and the confines of the Empire rose from 37 to 66 kilometres in the first century. Take, for example, the city of *Durocortorum* (Reims), capital of Belgian Gaul and principal city of the Remi. The city's walls enclosed some 550 hectares. This regional capital was separated by great distances from the capitals of bordering territories: 218 kilometres from *Augusta Treverorum* (Trier, Germany), with a surface area of 200 hectares; 175 kilometres from *Divodurum Mediomatricorum* (Metz), with a surface area of 50 hectares; and 225 kilometres from *Atuatuca Tungrorum*, with a surface area of 136 hectares. The 'urban fabric' was comprised of more than cities alone; it was a network of urban-type settlements, such as Nizy-le-Comte of the Remi (Reims), Bliesbruck of the Mediomatrici (Metz), Neumagen of the Treveri (Trier), and Maastricht of the Tungri (Tongeren), placed under the legal and political control of capital cities.

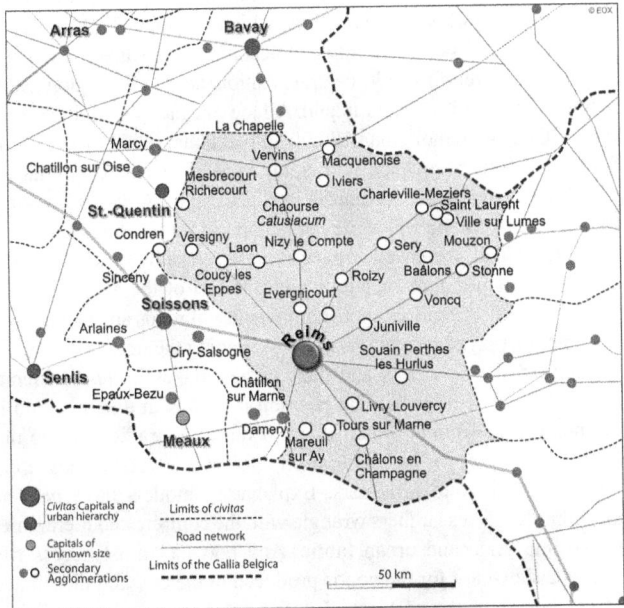

Figure 4.2 Network of towns in the *civitas* of Remi, including its capital of Durocortorum (Reims) and secondary settlements.

Sources: González-Villaescusa, 2010; Guillerat et al., 2020. Base map: Graticule. Infographics: © Vidal-Ros EOX.

Settlements and commerce evolved in the same ecosystem. Long-distance trade required coordinated access to distant markets in order to stimulate the production and circulation of raw materials and consumer goods. Land routes and, to an even greater extent, maritime and fluvial transport facilitated communication throughout the empire. Ports were so important in terms of trade networks that, according to Vitruvius, they played a key role in urban centrality. The location of a port could influence the foundation of a city (Vitruvius, *De architectura*, I, 5, 1) and condition the placement of the *forum*, pulling it from the city centre toward the port (I, 7, 1). This was certainly the case in coastal cities, such as the African cities of Sabratha and *Leptis Magna*, Pompeii, and certain port cities on the Seine, such as *Iuliobona* (Lillebonne).

Port cities were part of an integrated system and had all the same characteristics as land-based networks. They were a subset of the larger urban network and, by virtue of their location, occupied an important place in the network's hierarchy – one which required a high degree of infrastructure and public facilities to accommodate ships, merchants, and goods. This reinforced its central position, both in the region and in relation to other cities further inland. All the 'megacities' of the Roman Empire (those with more than 100,000 inhabitants), with the exception of *Apamea*, were associated with some kind of maritime installation (e.g., Smyrna, Antioch, Alexandria, and Carthage). *Ephesus* was only 10 kilometres from the sea, while Pergamon and Rome, though some 30 kilometres inland, were well connected to the coast by waterways. The need to maintain communications with the rest of the Mediterranean resulted from more than the mere convergence of roads and waterways; social factors played a significant role in shaping the network.

Analysis of shipwrecks and their cargos makes it clear a hierarchy existed between ports. The position of goods in a ship's hold is evidence of the rational organisation of maritime traffic and the ties between producers (of agricultural products, ore ingots, dishes, etc.), merchant guilds, and freighters. Explanatory models have become more complex as researchers wrangle with the complicated hierarchies of maritime trade and urban fabric. Any port city must necessarily serve as a showcase for the goods produced in the city and distributed and shipped from the port, which also served as the point of arrival for incoming goods. Such exchanges connected the city to the rest of the empire.

2 Density

H. Inglebert estimates that the Roman Empire contained anywhere from 2,000 to 2,700 cities between the Augustan era and the 5th century AD. Regional distributions are telling. 40% of the cities were situated in the East, 20% on the Iberian Peninsula, 16% in Italy and Africa. In the extreme northwest of the Empire, in the Gauls and Germanies, only 8% of cities could be found, and in Roman Britain, just 1% (roughly 20 cities in total). The most heavily urbanised regions were found in the Middle East, in close proximity to the birthplace of the most ancient human cities.

Keeping in mind the distances that separated regional capitals, however, this map of urban densities bears further qualification. As a general rule, and to facilitate travel and communication, the distance between most settlements (i.e., between capitals or between capitals and secondary settlements) was approximately three miles or five kilometres – the equivalent of two hours by mule.

The most densely occupied areas were peppered with small *civitates*, at least one every 15 kilometres on average. This included Lazio and Etruria, Sicily, Northern Africa, the territory formerly controlled by Carthage, and the extreme south of the Iberian Peninsula. In the regions peripheral to these (the rest of the Iberian Peninsula, North Africa, *Gallia Narbonensis*, and the north and south of the Italian Peninsula), medium-sized cities were found every 40 kilometres. Finally, in the outermost circle, including Gaul, the south and south-east of Roman Britain, and areas close to the *limes*, we find cities every 70 kilometres or so, each with a very large territory. Obviously, such remoteness complicated governance, which is why, over time, a multitude of settlements were created in addition to regional capitals to complete the urban network.

At the end of the 2nd century AD, the areas of greatest urban density (see Figure 4.3) coincided with the ancient territories of Greek, Punic,

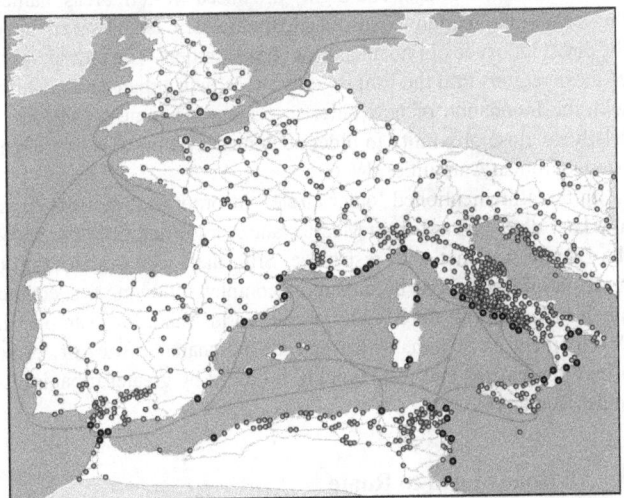

Figure 4.3 The Western Empire's main cities, Mediterranean ports (those cited more than three times by ancient sources), certain important ports of the Atlantic Ocean, as well as main roads and shipping routes.

Sources: Hanson, 2016; de Graauw et al., 2017; McCormick et al., 2013, and Arnaud, 2005. GIS: G. Davtian (CNRS-CEPAM); Infographics: E. Vidal-Ros (EOX).

and Etruscan influence. In other words, those with the longest urban traditions, dating back even to the Phoenicians (see Chapter 2). The eight cities of the empire with more than 100,000 inhabitants, besides Rome and the Phoenician settlement of Carthage, were close in proximity to the original foci of urban life, i.e., Asia Minor, Syria, Greece, and the Nile delta.

This diversity in the Roman urban fabric can be explained by the multiplicity of cultural substrates, the various integrative processes employed by the Empire, and the geopolitical evolution that occurred in these regions once brought into the Empire's fold. The average distance between cities in regions of the Mediterranean coastline urbanised prior to Romanisation was about 30 kilometres, whereas in the western provinces, and especially in the most remote areas of the Mediterranean, it was about 60 kilometres.

Thus, the areas with the greatest level of division into urban territories, like Sicily and Cyprus, also demonstrated the greatest level of interest from the great colonising societies of the first millennium, the Greeks and Phoenicians. The highly urbanised western areas, namely the south of the Iberian Peninsula and the Balearic Islands, were under the direct influence of Phoenician and Punic settlers. The incorporation of these regions into the Empire only made their urban fabric denser, with the foundation of new cities to accommodate new colonists in relatively close proximity to older settlements (Dionysius of Halicarnassus, Roman Antiquities, IV, 63).

In the aforementioned 'outer circle', incorporated into the empire at a later date, furthest from Mediterranean trade and little urbanised, the Empire was met with resistance. Still, the social organisation of these peripheral regions became more complex following first contact, albeit indirect, with the Mediterranean world. Take, for example, the development of *oppida*, which had all the characteristics of 'proto-urban' settlements and were quickly followed by greater urbanisation under Roman rule.

3 All Roads Lead to Rome

The first roads connecting Rome to the rest of the Italian peninsula date back to the 4th century BC. From that moment onward, travel times were greatly reduced. Geographical knowledge and representations of space, despite the simplicity of 'maps' and the linearity of the *Itineraria*, made it possible to estimate distance, foresee stopping points, and

The Empire's Urban Relays 51

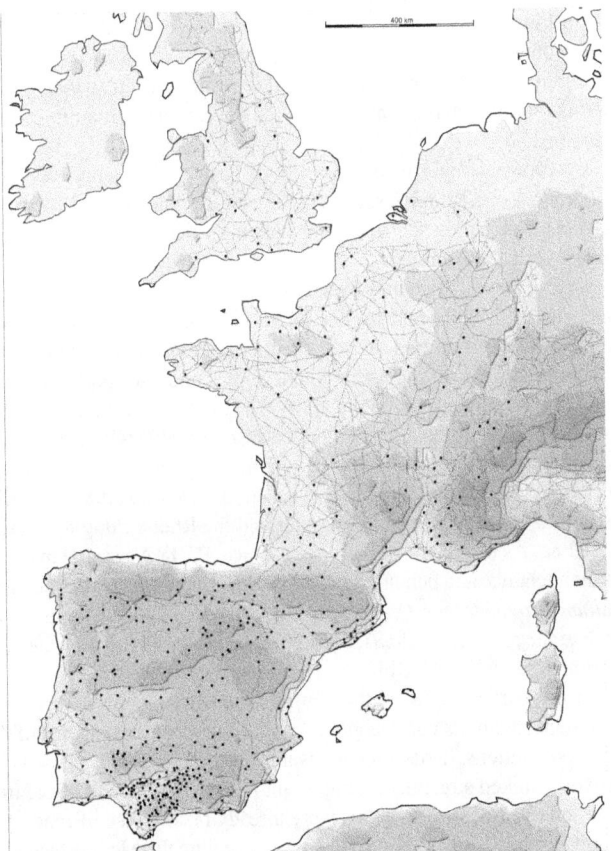

Figure 4.4 Network of principal towns and main roads in *Hispania, Gallia, Germania,* and *Britannia*.

Source: McCormick et al., 2013. GIS: L. Costa (CNRS – ArScAn). Base map: Graticule. Infographics: © Vidal-Ros EOX.

understand the overall organisation of terrestrial and maritime travel. The fall of Carthage in 146 BC, and the increasingly widespread use of *pozzolan* concrete (obtained from the basaltic rock of Campania) in the building of dikes, seawalls (*fauces portus*), and anchorages (Vitruvius, *De Architectura*, V, 12), helped bolster maritime transport. This is well demonstrated by an increase in the number of shipwrecks identified by maritime archaeologists, which reached its peak at this time. Ever more numerous, ports and lighthouses were the result of investments by commercial corporations and cities themselves. All this helped facilitate transportation and spurred the development of an integrated economy.

By coordinating a whole network of terrestrial, fluvial, and maritime routes, the Romans succeeded in simplifying transport dramatically. In connecting the great transloading river ports of the Rhone Valley with the Mediterranean, Arles was transformed into a major *emporion*, serving as a relay for the flow of commercial goods between Gaul and the Mediterranean. The canals constructed by the Romans to connect seas and rivers testify to their ability to transform the natural environment and tie together various routes and transport networks. Not only did this infrastructure allow the Romans to construct shorter routes, but it also helped make investments profitable with the application of lucrative tolls, the profits of which went to the *civitates* and supported their maintenance and civic functions. This was the case of the *fossa Mariana* (between Fos-sur-Mer and the Rhone), dug by Marius in 102 BC. As noted by Strabo (Geographica, IV, 1), Marseille oversaw its maintenance and benefited from the tolls. Likewise, the *municipium Aelium Cananefatium* (Voorburg, Netherlands) likely owes its existence to the *fossa Corbulonis*, built 20 years earlier (47 AD) by General Corbulon, between the Rhine and the Meuse estuary.

In the earliest days of the Empire, land routes played the most important role in its construction. Armies, their supplies, agents of the state, populations, herds, and goods all travelled overland. These large networks linked strategically important regions. At the end of the Iron Age and even before, societies were already making use of roads and highways, notably the great roadways connecting the Mediterranean to the Baltic, which carried luxury goods (such as coral, amber, furs, and slaves) and facilitated travel between places of regional or local interest. Rome understood their importance, and many of its routes, albeit larger, were grafted onto existing ones, which were thus integrated into a larger network and participated in the interests of the Roman world system. The *via Domiziana*, completed at the end of the 2nd century BC and described to us by Cicero (*Pro Fonteio*, VIII, 18), and the *Via Agrippa* of the 1st century BC, mentioned by Strabo (*Geographica*, IV, 6, 11), allowed the Romans to overcome certain accidents of topography by way of new technologies, diverse infrastructure, boundary markings, and the undertaking of large-scale civil engineering projects. In this way, new connections were made between existing road networks and their distances reinscribed within the empire's new scale. Likewise, many existing cities within those networks maintained their strategic importance, albeit on a larger geopolitical scale. Colonies were founded in response to the specific needs of regional points of strategic interest (e.g. crossroads, bridgeheads, and bottlenecks). Such was the case of Narbonne, at the crossroads of the *Via Domiziana*, which connected Italy to Spain, and other roads that led to the Garonne and on to the Atlantic Ocean. Cities were sometimes displaced by several kilometres to better serve as waystations in the new road system; others still were simply abandoned, considered too far removed from the main routes. Of course, some cities, like *Andemantunnum* (Langres) and *Durocortorum* (Reims), fit easily into the Roman network and did not move from where they had originally been founded.

Local communities and their leaders or *aediles* were responsible for maintaining the major roads of the *cursus publicus* and also organised, financed, and built regional networks. Take, for example, the famous Alcántara Bridge in Spain, built at the beginning of the 1st century under Emperor Trajan. Its construction involved the participation of no fewer than 11 cities of the province of Lusitania (CIL, II, 760).

Understandably, the price of imported goods varied as a function of the network and its infrastructure. When passing from one customs zone to another, merchants had to pay the *portorium* – a system of taxes and customs duties. Analysis of the Edict on Maximum Prices (*Edictum de pretiis rerum venalium*) has made it possible to determine the cost of maritime, river, and land transport within the Empire. Compared to transport by sea, transport downriver was seven times more expensive; transport upriver, 21 times more expensive; and transport over land, 49 times more expensive! Merchants were not the only ones reliant on this network. To function well – that is, to connect people and foster the adoption of its institutions – an empire must deal with the formidable problem of distance. In Rome, the institution of the *vehiculatio* (known later as the *cursus publicus*) was the consequence of profound territorial and administrative reforms undertaken during the time of Augustus (Suetonius, *Divus Augustus*, XLIX, 6). Placed under the direct jurisdiction of first the emperor and then the praetorian prefect, this institution was essential to the movement of the

Empire's functionaries, taxes, and goods. Communication between the head of the Empire (the emperor and Rome) and its provinces (the provincial capitals and their governors) followed a strict protocol in both directions. That said, the maintenance of the roads, the *stationes* (post offices), and the costs of personnel and beasts of burden all fell, as we have seen, not to the empire but to the *civitates*, who also benefited greatly from these routes.

4 Urbanism beyond the *Pomœrium*

In describing the suburbs of Rome, Dionysius of Halicarnassus (*Roman Antiquities*, IV, 13, 4) comments with astonishment on the fact that the city's growth occurred without interruption beyond the ramparts, such that an untrained observer could easily misinterpret the city's true size. This was not the case with most cities. The *pomœrium* occasioned an interruption – but one which differed from the urban discontinuity highlighted earlier (see *supra*, Chapter 3). Also called the *posimerium* or *promurium* ('nearest to the wall'), it defined a boundary and, in the eyes of the *pontifices*, the space within this boundary. The *urbs* was thus the space surrounded by the *pomœrium*, where urban (as opposed to military) auspices ruled.

The rural region outside this boundary was organised around and closely tied to the city by the major roadways extending from its gates that enabled it to communicate with its territory and the rest of the world. P. Arnaud spoke of a 'radiating, star-shaped model' ('*modèle rayonnant en étoile*') as a function of distance from the *pomœrium*. The first 500 *passus* (a 'half-*mille*', approximately 736 metres) beyond the ramparts, the *continentia*, was still considered part of the city. These were inhabited suburbs similar in nature to the nearby urban space. From a half-*mille* to 1 *mille* (approximately 736m to 1.5km) beyond the *pomœrium* were the *suburbia* and the *horti*. From 1 *mille* to 1.5 *milles* (approximately 1.5–2.2 km) were the *fundi suburbani*: rural spaces less than an hour's ride by donkey or cart. Beyond 1.5 *milles*, the countryside began. Finally, the distances between cities or between cities and neighbouring towns was typically 3 *milles* (5 km).

Beyond the suburbs (i.e., more than the minimum distance of 500 paces beyond the *pomœrium* set forth by the *Lex Ursonensis*), roads were frequently lined with tombs and followed the same radiating model. Often, the growth of the city occurred at the expense of these necropolises. There are at least two known examples where the construction of a public building resulted in the 'desacralisation' of funerary spaces. The first, around the middle of the 2nd century, was the Roman Circus of *Segobriga* (Saelices, Spain), which required the relocation of several tombs (an *impietas* counterbalanced through sacrificial offerings). The second, the construction of the ramparts enclosing the city of Triers (Germany) between 169 and 170 AD, resulted in the abandonment and displacement of funerary spaces situated along its path.

Outside the city, other sanctuaries were built in honour of eastern deities. But most of all, it was the burial places of the first Christians in ancient peripheral necropolises, associated with *martyria*, which gave rise to the first suburbs of late antiquity.

All these spaces served to divide up the city beyond the *pomœrium*, without interrupting the larger urban continuity. There is no sign of segregation between the city and its periphery; the periphery was a reproduction of the city-centre, albeit absent certain civic functions. As indicated by the *Lex Ursonensis* (CIL, ii, 5439) and confirmed by archaeological remains, certain economic activities were relegated to these areas, like those involving (for reasons of safety) the use of fire. Stone quarries, brick and tile kilns, pottery and tablet workshops, and tanning stations also found a place in the 'industrial zone' near the city. That said, the population itself often lived in large houses that made use of thermal baths, making them just as risky.

These spaces provided a kind of transition to the countryside and were crowned by a series of small vegetable and poultry farms (*fundi suburbani*), which were essential to the city and supplied its markets (see Chapter 5).

River ports and warehouses for incoming and outgoing goods and commodities were often found in close proximity, and such public infrastructure was typical of the *loca suburbana*. Ports, with their particular infrastructure, often occasioned a discontinuity in the urban fabric. In some cases, like Tarragona, a city's proximity to the coastline meant such installations were located in the *suburbium*. In other cases, distance only added to the discontinuity. Still in *Hispania Tarraconensis*, the *Portus Ilicitanus (Santa Pola)*, as noted by Ptolemy (II, 6, 14), was located roughly 15 kilometres from the colony of *Ilici* (Elche, Spain). Excavations have also brought to light a port from the Iberian period that later became the centre of a small neighbourhood, following colonial 'deductions' during the 1st century BC. It's also worth mentioning the *Portus Herculis Monoecus* (Monaco), located about

20 kilometres west of *Albintimilium* (Ventimiglia, Italy), probably the main port of that *civitas*. A small settlement in the west of the territory, this port served in Roman times as a customs post for the *portorium* of the *Quadragesima Galliarum*, a tax of 2.5% on the value of all merchandise passing from Italy to Gaul and vice-versa.

Some port settlements were also called *vicus* – a usage which, while explicit, is nonetheless difficult to interpret. For Gaul, we know of three inscriptions from Nantes, *Portus Namnetum* (CIL, XIII, 3105–3107), where the name includes both the ethnonym and the words *vicus portensis*. This expression either makes reference to a suburb, as argued by Y. Le Bohec, or else may represent one of the rare cases in which a *vicus* also served as regional capital, as suggested by M. Tarpin.

Finally, settlements that resulted from extraterritorial military activity and which were placed under the protection of legionary camps should be seen as representing both a civic and spatial – i.e., topological and topographic – discontinuity, albeit definitively urban in nature. Two types of such settlements can be distinguished, as demonstrated by *Carnuntum* in modern-day Austria and *Legio* in modern-day Spain. The first corresponds to an area known as the '*cannabae*', or civil suburbs, immediately adjacent to the military camp (Bad Deutsch-Altengburg or that of *Legio*, Leon). In the second case, military settlements have been identified at one *leuga* (one league of 2.2 kilometres, equivalent to 1.5 *milles*) from the legionary camps: at Petronell in the case of *Carnuntum*, and at Puente Castro (*ad Legionem*) in the case of *Legio*. Other examples are well documented, including the contiguous settlements of the camps of Vindolanda (United Kingdom) and Strasbourg (*Argentoratum*).

Bibliography

Andreau, J., Conclusions du dossier. Pour l'étude des entrepôts antiques, *Antiquités africaines*, 43, 2007, pp. 261–264.

Arnaud, P., Vers une définition géodynamique des *suburbia*: Eléments pour une zonation des zones péri-urbaines, in R. Bedon (ed.), *Suburbia. Les faubourgs en Gaule romaine et dans les régions voisines*, Caesarodonum, XXXII, 1998, pp. 63–81.

Arnaud, P., *Les Routes de la navigation antique. Itinéraires en Méditerranée et mer Noire*, Paris, Errance, 2005.

Baroni, A. F., Bernard, G., Le Teuff, B., Ruiz Darasse, C., *Echanger en Méditerranée. Acteurs, pratiques et normes dans les mondes anciens*, Rennes, Presses Universitaires de Rennes, 2016.

Crogiez-Pétrequin, S., Heller, A. (dirs.), *Empires connectés? La circulation de l'information dans les empires*, Bruxelles, P.I.E. Peter Lang, 2018.

De Graauw, A. *et al.*, Geodatabase of Ancient Ports and Harbors, in *DARMC Scholarly Data Series*, Cambridge, Center for Geographic Analysis, Harvard University, 2017 [Online: www.ancientportsantiques.com].

De Laet, S. J., *Portorium: Étude sur l'organisation douanière chez les Romains, surtout à l'époque du Haut-Empire*, Bruges, De Tempel, 1949.

Deru, X., Louvion, C., Les techniques de construction du second forum de Bavay (Nord): Utilisation, origine et datation des matériaux en terre cuite, *Gallia*, 76, 2019, pp. 45–81.

Dessaint, M., Variabilité des sources et biais scientifiques: Le cas du territoire des Rèmes, in E. Caron-Laviolette, N., Matomou-Adzo, C. Millot-Richard, B. Ramé (eds.), *Biais, hiatus et absences en archéologie*, Paris, Éditions de la Sorbonne, 2019 [Online: https://doi.org/10.4000/books.psorbonne.19438].

France, J., *Quadragesima Galliarum: L'organisation douanière des provinces alpestres, gauloises et germaniques de l'Empire Romain (Ier siècle avant J.-C. – IIIe siècle après J.-C.)*, Rome, Ecole Française de Rome, 2001.

France, J., Nelis-Clément, J. (eds.), *La statio. Archéologie d'un lieu de pouvoir dans l'Empire romain*, Bordeaux, Ausonius, 2014.

González-Villaescusa, R., Reims capitale de la Gaule Belgique et le réseau des villes de la province. Un essai, in R. González Villaescusa, J. Ruiz de Arbulo (eds.), *Simulacra Romae II*, Reims, Bulletin de la Société archéologique champenoise, Mémoire n° 19, 2010, pp. 201–206.

González Villaescusa, R., Padrino Fernández, S., Gayet, F., *Portus Herculis Monœcus*. Une agglomération portuaire aux portes de la Gaule, *Bulletin du Musée d'Anthropologie préhistorique de Monaco*, 59, 2019–2020, pp. 157–195.

Guillerat, N., Scheid, J., Melocco, M., *Infographie de la Rome antique*, Paris, Passés Composés, 2020.

Hanson, J. W., *An Urban Geography of the Roman World, 100 BC to AD 300*, Oxford, Archaeopress, 2016.

Hanson, J. W., *Cities Database* [Online: oxrep.classics.ox.ac.uk/databases/cities/].

Houten, P. V., *Urbanisation in Roman Spain and Portugal: Civitates Hispaniae in the Early Empire*, London – New York, Routledge, 2021.

Inglebert, H., Le monde romain et la civilisation romaine, in H. Inglebert (ed.), *Histoire de la civilisation romaine*, Paris, Presses Universitaires de France, 2005, pp. 33–75.

Kort, J. W. de, Raczynski-Henk, Y., The *Fossa Corbulonis* between the Rhine and Meuse Estuaries in the Western Netherlands, *Water History*, 6, 2014, pp. 51–71.

Laurence, R., Cleary, S. E., Sears, G., *The City in The Roman West c. 250 BC – c. AD 250*, Cambridge, Cambridge University Press, 2011.

McCormick, M., *et al.*, Roman Road Network (Version 2008), in *DARMC Scholarly Data Series*, Cambridge, Center for Geographic Analysis, Harvard University, 2013 [Online: https://doi.org/10.7910/DVN/TI0KAU].

Morillo Cerdán, A., García Marcos, V., Un ejemplo particular de comunidad cívica en territorio militar: El *vicus* de *Ad legionem* (Puente Castro, León), in E. Ortiz de Urbina (coord.), *Ciudadanías, Ciudades y Comunidades Cívicas en Hispania (de los Flavios a los Severos)*, Sevilla, Universidad de Sevilla, 2019.

Purcell, N., Urban Spaces and Central Places, in S. E. Alcock, R. Osborne (dir.), *Classical Archaeology*, Oxford, Blackwell, 2007, pp. 182–202.

Rousse, C., Fontaine, S., Landure C., Marty, F. Quesnel Y., Vella, C., Dussouliez P., Fleury J., Uheara M., *Le canal de Marius: Réflexions autour d'une nouvelle hypothèse de tracé dans le secteur des Marais du Vigueirat*, Revue archéologique de Narbonnaise, 52, 2019, pp. 109–120.

Santrot, J., Au temps d'*Argiotalus*, Nantes, Rezé et le port des Namnètes, *Annales de Bretagne et des Pays de l'Ouest*, 115(1), 2008, pp. 55–97.

5 Economic Autonomy

1 The Agricultural Territories of Roman Cities

The basic territorial unit of the Roman Empire was not the city itself, but the city and its territory, the *civitas*. Indeed, cities required land to produce the vast majority of what their citizens consumed. Moreover, the Roman city was nothing more than the common place of residence of the great landowners of the surrounding countryside. This is especially clear when one observes that the *civitas* comprised the legal context for all those who enjoyed '*jus civitas*', or citizenship, in that the *civitas* was a whole formed from one or more settlements and the surrounding territory. As a result, the aristocracy that resided there was both urban and rural in nature and enjoyed a kind of double residence – that of the city and that of their individual rural properties or *villae*. In addition, by integrating the greater part of a *civitas*' population, including all the small landowners of the countryside, into a single fiscal system, this cellular territorial model left little room for autonomy among the peasantry.

The city was a major centre of consumption, and it could only remain self-sufficient thanks to its territory. The demand for local products grew steadily with the ongoing rural exodus caused by the proliferation of urban centres, greater specialisation of labour, and the presence of a growing population of workers and craftsmen who lived within the city but didn't directly produce what they consumed. Edible gardens encircling the city were one spatial consequence of the unique composition of this urban population, as evidenced by the remains of tree crops found in and around, for example, the city of *Durocortorum* (Reims). The rearing of small animals for food (a practice known as *villatica pastio*), described by Varro (*De agricultura*, III) as a novelty in his time (the second half of the 1st century), was another solution

DOI: 10.4324/9781003450856-6

to increasing urban demands. It supplied the urban market with a long list of products, including but not limited to poultry, mammals, sea and freshwater fish, molluscs, and honey.

The practice of *pastio agrestis*, on the other hand, developed not on the urban periphery but in the *saltus*. This space, typically found at the fringe of a *civitas*' territory, was comprised of forests (*silvae*) and pastures (*pastiones*) given over to livestock. It was often a relic of small peasant estates and common grounds (*communiones*). Here, livestock moved freely between the environmental niches that predated the territorial organisation of the *civitas*. Joaquín Gómez-Pantoja sees this as one explanation for the conflicts that arose, following colonisation at the start of the 2nd century BC, that pitted Roman troops against members of the Hispanic *Lusitani* and Italian *Pecuarii*, who were viewed by Rome as bandits – and not simply transhumant shepherds. It is likely these spatial competitions were resolved by the granting of pasturages far beyond the limits of the *civitas*. A milestone found 200 kilometres from the capital of the colony of *Ucubi* (Espejo, Spain) in Baetica, for example, is believed to mark the divide between the colon's territory and that of *Emerita Augusta* (Mérida) in Lusitania (*CIL*, II, 656).

Most of the basic necessities, though, were produced in the *ager*: a cleared space meant for farming. A good part of the population's needs was met by cereals. Thanks to the *Cura Annonae* (the free distribution of grain in Rome), we know the approximate monthly consumption of grain per citizen was about 5 *modii* or 35 kilograms of wheat. As noted by M. Tarpin, the question is an important one, considering the time frames involved in the foundation of a colony and the ability to properly feed a population.

Finally, the question of protein was equally vital. Indeed, not everyone had access to the products of the *pastio villatica*. Research has shown that the most common source of protein, Varro's 'food of the people' (*De Agricultura*, III), was preserved fish in all its forms: *garum*, *allex*, *liquamen*, and others. Salted, smoked, and various other preparations of fish were exported in *amphorae* across the Mediterranean. As the empire expanded, they were adopted in more northern regions and adapted to oceanic fish from the coasts of Gaul and even Brittany. In fact, urban consumption of cured fish was so significant that studies of the ichthyofauna of *Londinium* (London) have revealed a direct correlation between the consumption of cod and the very existence of the city, from its foundation in the middle of the 1st century AD to the collapse of urban life at the beginning of the 5th century AD, when evidence of its consumption dries up.

2 Urban Production

This close connection between landowners and city elites eliminated any kind of segregation between urban spaces and the storage and transformation of raw materials, such as pottery, textiles, and marquetry, associated with commercial activity. In late Republican cities, each *domus* was furnished with a *taberna* which opened onto the street and allowed the sale of products. These stalls were often located on main roads, as in Pompeii and Ostia. Progressively, however, from the 1st century AD onward and especially during the 2nd century AD, this practice fell out of fashion. From this point on, fewer of the sumptuous *domus* show evidence of commercial activity, which seems to have been relegated to more humble residences. This was certainly the case in *Durocortorum* (Reims), where such 'productive units' became concentrated between the two great roads running north and south along the river Vesle, in close proximity to the port that linked Reims to the rest of Gaul. Indeed, the remains of an artisanal zone have been found here with a variety of objects directly related to the production and processing of fabrics and cloth, including weaving cellars, loom weights, alum used as dyeing mordant, and fuller's earth and chalk used to degrease wool. The *Notitia Dignitatum* (List of Offices) also mentions (XI) the existence of a *Procurator gynaecii Remensis* ('Manager of the weaving factory of Reims').

This especially well-documented example was hardly an exception. The Hispanic cities of *Baelo Claudia* (Bolonia), *Carteia* (San Roque), *Emporion* (Ampurias), as well as *Tipasa* in Algeria, were dotted with salting factories – despite the powerful odour they would have produced. Likewise, the so-called '*bottega del garum*' – the Pompeiian salting store – was not simply a storefront but also an *officina salsamentaria*, where Pompeiian *garum* was actually made, as noted by Pliny (*Naturalis historia*, XXXI, 44) and confirmed by the research of D. Bernal. The same can be said of the olive presses of *Volubilis* (Morocco) in Mauretania Tingitana. The presence of about 50 of them, distributed throughout the city, shows that this activity was anything but infrequent.

As we have seen, the more dangerous productive activities, such as those using fire, were relegated to the outskirts of the city (without being completely absent from urban centres, as in Reims). Pottery workshops that produced table and kitchenware, known as figlinae, as well as tile, glass, and metallurgic (e.g., bronzers' and blacksmiths') workshops are well attested by the archaeological record (in Alesia and Autun, for example) and, very frequently, by inscriptions testifying to the existence of professional colleges. As urban centres themselves, a good number of secondary settlements played host to artisanal activities. This was the case of the *vicus* of *Condatomagus* in *La Graufesenque* (Millau), where large workshops produced South Gaulish *terra sigillata* tableware, distributed throughout Gaul, Spain, and Mauretania Tingitana.

3 Urban Consumption

The question of production and consumption goes well beyond the territorial framework of the *civitas*, inviting us to consider 'external' trade as well as certain forms of urban consumption that developed as the city itself became a locus of commercial exchange.

Some of these forms, we shall see, concern not only the city but also *villae* and military camps. In the city of *Durocortorum* (Reims), carpological vestiges in large seignorial residences have made it possible to identify supply systems that extended far beyond the surrounding countryside. In a similar fashion, the presence of cod in the city of *Londinium* (London) seems to have had a far more distant origin than mere coastal fishing. The oysters and shellfish found in territories devoid of such resources, like in the centre of Gaul, were necessarily transported and distributed well beyond the territories of the *civitates* that produced them.

Remains of earthenware have allowed English researchers to identify a variety of different ceramic styles. These include Italic forms found in colonies and military camps as well as imported forms and local interpretations thereof – particularly in small towns, where local elites adopted 'Roman' styles of living.

Likewise, some *villae* adopted the *habitus* of urban consumption. For example, while bovines on farms were consumed at an advanced age after serving as draught animals, on seigneurial estates, they were consumed at a much younger age. On the sites of these same *villae*, it is not uncommon to find *amphorae* that once contained wine, oil, or fish sauce from distant markets – even when such things could easily have been produced on-site instead. Of course, the *villae* imported more than just food. Stone and terracotta, decorative standards and marble, and motifs of painted plaster or mosaics – all the ostentatious trappings of administrative life associated with the *aediles* were procured from itinerant workshops.

In fact, the *aediles* were well known for this kind of conspicuous urban consumption. Architecture is an essential component of urbanism, and its degree of sophistication is a faithful indicator of the quality of urban life. In the words of P. Gros, the *imperium* can be found by way of *aedificatio* and *urbanitas*. So much so that, in the subsoil of modern cities, the stratigraphic layer corresponding to the period of Roman urban society is measured in cubic metres of ashlar, mortar, and architectural terracotta, while the subsoil corresponding to the end of the Roman era, from the 4th and 5th centuries AD, is what's known as 'dark earth': soil with a high organic content, signifying that stone and brick constructions were replaced with farms, pasturages, and buildings made of perishable materials.

The construction of the Empire's most prestigious buildings required great quantities of sandstone and limestone for ashlar and clay for bricks, tiles, and architectural terracotta. This is why, at least in principle, most quarries belonged to a *civitas*, with the notable exception of those that produced building stones of a unique and exceptional quality, such as marble from *Luna* (Luni, Italy) and porphyry from *Mons Porphyrites* (Egypt). These passed directly into the hands of the State. That being said, we know these exceptional materials were also commercialised, as they have been found in public buildings of both imperial and municipal construction. Freshly excised blocks have also been found in shipwrecks near the coast. Many of these stone quarries, some of whose resources are still exploited to this day, left an indelible mark on the landscape. Take for example El Mèdol in *Tarraco* (Tarragona, Spain), used in the construction of the city's aqueduct and circus; or Estel, in the territory of *Nemausus* (Nîmes), used in the construction of the aqueduct that contains the famous *Pont du Gard*.

It was the construction of these temples, warehouses, ports, baths, theatres, amphitheatres, circuses, forums, basilicas, and *curiae* which contributed to the thick sediment left by ancient Roman cities. Even beyond the city, such as with dams, bridges, and aqueducts, they participated in urban life by facilitating communications within the Roman urban network. The financing of *munera* (public works or sites) by wealthy citizens shows that there was a clear relationship between a settlement's *aediles* and the economic dynamics of its region. Any time the local economy went into crisis and economic activity weakened, these acts of euergetism became noticeably rarer, and the maintenance of buildings worsened, eventually resulting in their ruin and definitive abandonment. Monumental buildings commissioned by the *aediles* thus doubtless contributed to the economic dynamism of the Empire's *civitates*. C. Rico has estimated, for example, that the quantity of bricks used in the construction of the ramparts of the city of *Tolosa* (Toulouse) between 20 and 30 AD numbered approximately 10 million. The same bricks, formed using the same mould, were used in other contemporary constructions of public (the amphitheatre and the aqueduct) and private (urban *domus* and *villae*) nature.

While the sheer diversity of urban buildings is remarkable (see Chapter Six), one of them bears closer examination: the *macellum*. A symbol of urban consumption, this market of sorts had a specific function: the sale of provisions and foodstuffs to the city. Their appearance followed the gradual removal of merchants and commercial activities from the Roman forum at the end of the 3rd century BC. The first known example in Rome dates back to 179 BC and was inspired by a Hellenistic model. Various meats, poultry, game, and cold cuts could be found here, as well as fish and seafood – in short, many of the high-yield products mentioned by Varro (see Chapter 5.1. The Agricultural Territories of Roman Cities). Though their construction was often an act of euergetism by nobles and members of the imperial house, they were managed by *civitates*, and the freshness and weight of products was strictly regulated. The presence of *mensae ponderariae* – stone 'conversion tables' with official weights and measurements – was indispensable. The table in the market of *Leptis Magna* (Khoms, Libya) offers one good example, with the lengths of the Egyptian cubit, Punic cubit, and Roman foot clearly marked for all to see and use. Bronze standards served as a reference of various common measurements for the market's regular customers.

4 Financial Autonomy

Given their importance in the Roman state's fiscal system, *civitates* possessed a large degree of financial autonomy. A complex fiscal system ensured land within the *civitas* rarely escaped its control. Exceptions existed, but they were just that, and the relation between territorial fiscality and civic territoriality has been well demonstrated by M. Corbier. Of course, the Empire still needed to take stock of its territorial holdings in a standardised way, and it did so via the *census*, an inventory of citizens and their property taken every five years. But the basic unit of the *census* within each province was none other than the *civitas*, each of which was responsible for collecting taxes on behalf of Rome (*civitas, conventus, provincia*).

The Empire's fiscal system relied on the smooth functioning of this one fundamental unit and its control over the surrounding territory and resources. Citizens' administrative, legal, and political needs, in turn, were met by the city. Everything served to reinforce a *civitas*' control over its territory and maintain the imbalance of power between the one and the other, between city elites and peasants, between wealthy landowners and villagers.

Most of a *civitas*' revenue came from the renting of land and the sale of rights of access to pastures under its control (and thus in the public domain). But it was also generated, albeit to a lesser extent, from indirect taxes levied on the exchange of goods, such as market and anchorage rights, revenue from public baths, 'honorary sums' paid by elected officials following election (for decurions and magistrates), and liturgies or *munera*: public works and festivals sponsored by wealthy citizens for the benefit of the population.

The territory of the *civitas* was the source of not only the wealth of its inhabitants but also the income necessary for the smooth operation of the state and the army. This wealth was concentrated primarily in cities and in the hands of urban elites to the detriment of the rest of the territory, further reinforcing the inequality and imbalance between city and countryside.

Bibliography

Akerraz, A., Lenoir, M., Les huileries de Volubilis, *Bulletin d'Archéologie Marocaine*, XIV, 1981–1982, pp. 69–101.

Andreau, J., Quelques observations sur les *macella*, in V. Chankowski, P. Karvonis (eds.), *Tout vendre, tout acheter. Structures et équipements des marchés antiques. Actes du colloque d'Athènes, 16–19 juin 2009*, Ausonius – École française d'Athènes, Bordeaux – Athènes, 2012, pp. 75–82.

Bardot-Cambot, A., Coquillages des villes et coquillages des champs: Une enquête en cours, in X. Deru, R. Gonzalez-Villaescusa (dirs.), *Consommer dans les campagnes de la Gaule romaine. Actes du Xe congrès de l'Association AGER, Revue du Nord. Hors série*, Lille, 2014, pp. 109–120.

Bernal, D., Cottica, D., Produzione e vendita di pesce sotto sale e suoi derivati a Pompei nel 79 d.C.: Le evidenze dalla cosiddetta "Bottega del *garum*" (I, 12, 8), in R. González-Villaescusa, K. Schörle,

F. Gayet, F. Rechin (dirs.), *L'exploitation des ressources maritimes de l'Antiquité. Activités productives et organisation des territoires, XXVIIe rencontres internationales d'archéologie et d'histoire d'Antibes & XIIe colloque de l'association AGER*, Antibes, APDCA, 2017, pp. 235–251.

Bessac, J. C., Vacca-Goutoulli, M., La carrière romaine de L'Estel près du Pont du Gard, *Gallia*, 59, 2002, pp. 11–28.

Blanc, N., *Pullus, gallus* et *gallina*: Déclinaisons antiques, *Revue d'ethnoécologie*, 12, 2017, pp. 4–25.

Corbier, M., City, Territory and Taxation, in J. Rich, A. Wallace-Hadrill (eds.), *City and Country in the Ancient World*, London, Routledge, 1991, pp. 211–239.

Filippo, R. de, Rico, C., La forme et la marque: La brique à Toulouse au Ier siècle de notre ère, *Pallas*, 46, 1997, pp. 67–86.

Galinié, H., L'entre-deux des villes, in H. Galinié (dir.), *Tours antique et médiéval. Lieux de vie, temps de la ville. 40 ans d'archéologie urbaine*, Tours, FERACF, 2007, pp. 356–358.

Gómez-Pantoja, J., *Pastio agrestis*: Pastoralismo en Hispania romana, in J. Gómez-Pantoja, *Los rebaños de Gerión: Pastores y trashumancia en Iberia antigua y medieval*, Madrid, Casa de Velázquez, 2001, pp. 177–213.

González Villaescusa, R., Problématique archéologique sur la production de laine et d'étoffes en Gaule Belgique, in L. Pons Pujol (dir.), *Hispania et Gallia: Dos provincias del occidente romano*, Barcelona, Universitat de Barcelona, 2010, pp. 125–143.

Gutiérrez García-Moreno, A., López Vilar, J., La cantera de El Mèdol. Técnicas, organización y propuesta de evolución de la extracción del material lapídeo, in A. Gutiérrez Garcia-Moreno, P. Rouillard (eds.), *Lapidum natura restat. Canteras antiguas de la Península Ibérica*, Tarragona – Madrid, ICAC – Casa de Velázquez, 2018, pp. 67–80.

Hallier, G., Coudée, *Encyclopédie berbère*, 14, 1994, pp. 2111–2121 [Online: https://doi.org/10.4000/encyclopedieberbere.2334].

Jouhet, E., Brunet, M., Mathelart, P. Matterne, V., Activités artisanales sur la rive droite de la Vesle à Reims/Durocortorum, *Gallia*, 79(1), 2022, pp. 259–291.

Koehler, A., Vergers antiques dans les campagnes péri-urbaines: Le cas de Reims, in S. Lepetz, V. Matterne (dirs.), *Dossier: Cultivateurs, éleveurs et artisans dans les campagnes de Gaule romaine. Matières premières et produits transformés, Actes du VIe colloque AGER, Compiègne, du 5 au 7 juin 2002*, Amiens, Revue Archéologique de Picardie, 2003, pp. 37–46.

Lavoix, G., Gerber F., Guitton, D., De l'utile et de l'agréable: Un jardin romain chez les Pictons. La Viaube 1 à Jaunay-Clan (Vienne), *Gallia*, 73, 2016, pp. 81–106.

Mangin, M., Fluzin, P., L'organisation de la production métallurgique dans une ville gallo-romaine: Le travail du fer à Alésia, *Revue archéologique de l'Est*, 55, 2007, pp. 129–150.

Matterne, V., Économie végétale à partir des études carpologiques du boulevard Dr Henri-Henrot à Reims/Durocortorum, *Gallia*, 79, 2022, pp. 293–300.

Orton, D., Morris, J., Locker, A., Barrett, J., Fish for the city: Meta-Analysis of Archaeological Cod Remains and the Growth of London's Northern Trade, *Antiquity*, 88, 2014, 516–530.

Pitts, M., Globalisation, Circulation and Mass Consumption in the Roman World, in M. Pitts M. J. Versluys (eds.), *Globalisation and the Roman World. World History, Connectivity and Material Culture*, Cambridge, Cambridge University Press, 2015, pp. 69–98.

Poux, M., Produire et consommer dans l'arrière-pays colonial de *Lugdunum* et de Vienne: Étude de cas, in X. Deru, R. Gonzalez-Villaescusa (dirs.), *Consommer dans les campagnes de la Gaule romaine. Actes du Xe congrès de l'Association AGER*, Lille, Revue du Nord. Hors-série, 2014, pp. 323–356.

Tarpin, M., *Urbem condere/coloniam deducere*: La procédure de "foundation" coloniale, dans M. Tarpin (dir.), *Colonies, territoires et statuts: Nouvelles approches*, Suppléments aux *Dialogues d'Histoire Ancienne*, 23, 2021, pp. 13–94.

Vermeulen, F., Zuiderhoek, A. J., *Space, Movement and the Economy in Roman Cities in Italy and Beyond*, London – New York, Routledge, Taylor & Francis Group, 2021.

Whittaker, C. The Consumer City Revisited: The Vicus and the City, *Journal of Roman Archaeology*, 3, 1990, pp. 110–118.

6 The City and Its Spaces

1 Urbanitas

All the important decisions concerning the territory were made within the primary settlement, the capital city. Urban citizens knew they belonged to a different world. Though they derived their wealth from land holdings, it was in the city that they resided, and it was here that they spent the surplus generated as a result of agricultural activity. Likewise, though they may have earned an income from other industries, like trade, it was invariably reinvested into land. The intense level of communication, decision-making, and commercial exchange conferred upon the capital an undeniable pre-eminence over the rest of the territory. Products from the *ager* and, more generally, all the goods arriving from throughout the territory of the *civitas* – and those of other *civitates* – were stored in warehouses within the city and thereafter redistributed to the urban population.

The disparities in agrarian development between Rome and the populations its armies encountered as they advanced westward were probably not as great as between the *urbanitas* of Rome, other urbanised groups, and societies devoid of any urban traditions. Each newly conquered territory was incorporated into a single continuum to facilitate communication with the *caput mundi*. To do this, one or more urban centres were typically organised around a common civic unit, a central place where the members of the community could meet and create new relationships, make decisions, communicate, and engage in commerce. All this was carried out with a certain level of political autonomy. The citizenry thus needed a space to meet and for these spaces to have a clear meaning for the society as a whole. As suggested by the semiologist U. Eco, architecture is a signifier that speaks to the function or functions that occasioned a building's construction.

DOI: 10.4324/9781003450856-7

In this way, the existence of the citizenry presupposed a certain level of *urbanitas* and the existence of an appropriate architecture. But in regions where urban life was non-existent, Rome actively stimulated the integration of local populations into a *civitas* and the diffusion of a common set of cultural mores. In describing the government of Cnaeus Iulius Agricola in Brittany, Tacitus thoroughly explored the consequences of this relationship between urbanisation and Romanisation, the 'assimilating power of the symbols of *urbanitas*', in the words of P. Gros. But Tacitus, no doubt carried away in praise of his father-in-law, describes the latter as practically demiurgic: along with its institutions, it was the customs and traditions of Rome that were ultimately adopted. 'All this in their ignorance, they called civilisation, when it was but a part of their servitude' (*Agricola*, 21, trans. S. Bryant). What is most striking about Tacitus' account is how exhaustive it is. Among the buildings he mentions are temples, forums, residences, porticoes, and baths – all those spaces which correspond to the Vitruvian conception of the most important urban functions and where a new class of citizens could socialise and govern together. These were joined by spaces of leisure and domestic life, no less revealing of the Roman *art de vivre*: strolling under porticoes and frequenting baths – not to mention the language (Latin), the gastronomy, and the style of dress (the toga!).

2 Monumental Landscapes

Without getting lost in the details of the urban terrain characteristic of Roman and provincial cities, it bears reviewing certain architectural works, in light of the material traces left by their monumentalisation. For a clear picture, let us refer to P. Gros' comprehensive chapter in H. Inglebert's 'Nouvelle Clio'.

The multiplicity of Roman buildings within the same space testifies to the profound political and social transformations experienced by Roman society. Moreover, architectural styles themselves evolved as other cities entered the Roman fold. And not all buildings of the same name and same architectural layout served the same purpose. Such transformations were more important in the Empire's West than the East, steeped as it was in a long architectural tradition – although this didn't prevent the Athenian *agora* or the Corinthian *forum* in Greece from being transformed after their integration into the empire.

The public square, the forum, was gradually freed from the commercial and artisanal functions it originally served and was closed to the public at the end of the Republican period. With time, it became a controlled space, separating just a little further the elite from the rest of the population. Dominated by the basilica, the curia and, from the Principate onward, the dynastic temple, this space came to reflect the continuity between the two powers that mingled there: the reigning dynasty on the one hand and the local elites on the other.

Such closed forums acquired a critical importance in the later, peripheral provinces. This was the case of the tripartite, axial forums of Gaul, which adopted a closed configuration (*Durocortorum*, Reims; *Bagacum*, Bavay; *Augusta Treverorum*, Trier, Germany; *Aventicum*, Avenches, Switzerland), the forums of the Celtiberian regions in Spain (*Colonia Clunia Sulpicia*, Clunia; *Termes*, Tiermes; *Segobriga*, Saelices; *Conimbriga, Ebora Liberalitas Iulia*, Evora, Portugal) and the enclosed, square-like forums of Roman Britain (*Londinium*, London; *Calleva Atrebatum*, Silchester; *Venta Silurum*, Caerwent, England).

A city's theatre could often be found in close proximity to its forum. More than simple buildings that housed spectacles, these *ludi Scaenici* served as spaces of worship and political representation and were thus similar in function to temples. The stage wall was often adorned by a set of '*post scaenum*' porticos, a kind of covered gallery, as in the Theater of Pompey in Rome. During the time of the Julio-Claudian dynasty, the theatre replaced the forum as a central space, both geographically and politically. The examples of *Lugdunum* (Lyon), *Aventicum* (Avenches, Switzerland), and the colonies of *Arelate* (Arles), *Arausio* (Orange), and *Nemausus* (Nîmes) in *Gallia Narbonensis* are well known. Finally, F. Dumasy has shown how theatres and other ceremonial buildings formed 'sacred' and urban formations,[1] thoroughly integrated into the urban fabric to facilitate the circulation of religious processions.

As architectural points of interest continued to shift, the amphitheatre replaced forums and theatres as a central urban space from the end of the 2nd or early 1st century AD, during the Flavian dynasty. Its origins, however, go back even further. As early as the 2nd century BC, amphitheatres in Campania hosted gladiators and *venationes*. This architectural model spread, and the amphitheatre became a primary meeting place for the ruling class and the Roman people. The starting point of this remarkable diffusion was the Colosseum,

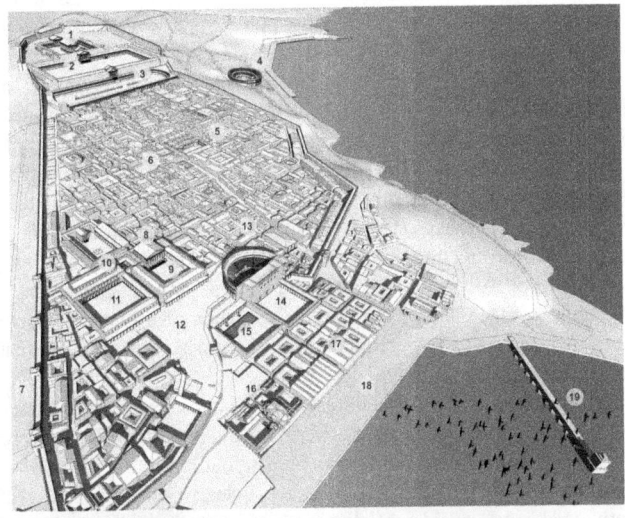

Figure 6.1 Roman city of *Tarraco* and main monuments: 1: Temple of Augustus, 2: Provincial Forum, 3: Circus, 4: Amphitheatre, 5: Public Baths, 6: Dwelling, 7: Walls, 8: Capitol, 9: Republican Forum, 10: Judicial Basilica; 11: Augustan Forum, 12: Open Commercial Area, 13: Theater, 14: Porticus post scaenam, 15: Nymphaeum, 16: Port Baths, 17: Warehouses (*horrea*), 18: Dock, 19: Pier on piles.

Sources: Volumetric restitution of Tarraco in the 2nd century AD, according to R. Mar, J. A. Beltrán Caballero, and J. Ruiz de Arbulo, Universitat Rovira i Virgili, Tarragona.

the *amphitheatrum Flavium* in Rome. It propagated throughout the empire, effecting transformations in the urban fabric. In some cases, a city's amphitheatre was built beyond the ramparts, which predated its construction, making it easier to attract people from all over the city.

In *Gallia Comata* ('Long-haired Gaul') and Britannia, as for example in Verulamium (St Albans), the amphitheatre adopted a hybrid form, known as a theatre-amphitheatre. It served both functions, thanks to a stage and an orchestra accompanied by *cavea* (bleachers), constituting three quarters of the building's circular form, and allowing for spectacles suitable to both theatres and amphitheatres. These theatre-amphitheatres were often built as part of a larger rural complex that brought together sanctuaries, theatres, and thermal baths. One example is that of Grand in Vosges, France, in the settlement of *Andesina*, *civitas* of the Leuci. In

Tres Galliae, these buildings were distributed among the capitals of *civitates*, some of which already had an amphitheatre, while theatres were scattered throughout other settlements and sanctuaries.

Several additional installations became popular starting in the 2nd century. Bathing complexes were one of these. As with amphitheatres, public thermal baths (*balnea)* and spaces for exercise (*Palestrae*) had existed for a long time. However, they gradually became more popular in Rome from the 1st century BC onwards, largely due to euergetism. As a result, they were open to all social classes and became important spaces for meeting and socialising. From the following century onwards, emperors and local elites helped transform baths into centres of public hygiene and physical exercise. Baths of different temperatures and steam rooms were laid out in such a way as to induce sweating and cleanse the skin.

From the earliest imperial initiatives, the largest examples of Roman baths spanned several hectares. Nero's baths measured two hectares in surface area; Trajan's thermal baths, four hectares; Caracalla's, 11 hectares, and Diocletian's, 14 hectares. Indeed, from Trajan onwards, baths tend to be considerably larger, primarily to accommodate libraries, conference rooms, and the like, with ample space on all sides for foot traffic. Similar examples can be found in the provinces: the baths of Vienna (0.3 hectares) and Edeta (*Lliria*, Spain; 0.5 hectares); the three thermal complexes of *Cemenelum* (Cimiez, Nice, France; 2 hectares); the baths of *Aquae Sulis* and the sanctuary in Bath (United Kingdom; 3.5 hectares); the *Barbarathermen* of *Augusta Treverorum* (Trier, Germany; 4 hectares); and finally, among the largest of the western provinces, the thermal baths of Cluny at *Lutetia* (Paris; 6.5 hectares). The construction of such facilities required not only large sums of money and complex building practices but also an abundant source of flowing water, brought to the city by means of one or more aqueducts, as well as vast quantities of wood for heating the pools and saunas.

The end of the 2nd century and the beginning of the next also saw the rise of the circus, the last great installation characteristic of Roman cities. Of course, not all cities had one, and not all races required a hippodrome; but the circus was the ideal space to host chariot races, as the required track had to measure between 300 and 500 metres. As with amphitheatres, the archetype is a Roman building, the *Circus Maximus* in Rome, which, at least structurally, existed from the 1st century BC onwards. Eager for this kind of entertainment, the people encouraged the construction of additional *circi* within the *Urbs*, paid for by the ruling class. Competitions between the various stables helped channel social tensions. Although there are examples of circuses outside of Rome from the 1st century onwards, most of them date from the 3rd and 4th centuries AD and follow the same architectural plan. These include the circus of *Arelate* (Arles), dating from the end of the 1st century; those of *Carthago* (Tunisia) and *Colonia Claudia Victricensis* (Colchester, U.K.), from the beginning of the 2nd century; *Saguntum* (Sagunto, Spain) from the 2nd or 3rd century; and that of *Sitifis* (Setif, Algeria).

Finally, a *macellum*, mentioned earlier, was an open-air courtyard, enclosed by a wall, to which a handful of stores were attached and within which sometimes stood one or two circular temples or *tholos*. Archaeological excavations have uncovered counters (tables for displaying measurements) and drainage channels for easy cleaning. The model spread beyond Italy to the provinces, starting with Spain in the 1st century BC, and especially to communities of high rank and areas where Romanisation was both precocious and intense, such as *Lugdunum Convenarum* in Saint-Bertrand-de-Comminges, whose *macellum* dates from the time of Tiberius. Likewise, there is the *macellum* of *Augusta Vindelicum* (Augsburg, Germany), dating from the first half of the 2nd century, and that of *Ratae Corieltauvorum* (Leicester, U.K.), built between the end of the 2nd century and the beginning of the 3rd.

3 The Urban Fabric and Its Roadways

To understand the urban fabric of a Roman city, we must first examine the organisation of its streets and other public routes. Harmony was achieved by ensuring that the roads that structured the territory and divided up the land, the *cardo* and *decumanus maximus*, shared the same orientation as the city (the *ratio pulcherrima*) and followed the correct ratios and proportions (Hyginus, *De limitibus constituendis*, 6, 7).

The first step taken by surveyors when founding a Greek or Roman city was naturally to establish a network of streets. In the West, the public spaces were delimited first, and the remainder set aside for private use (either rented, used by private individuals with authorisation, or else set aside for public buildings). Roads served as the interface between private and public space, facilitating traffic within the city and access to private property. Of course, they served multiple other functions, too.

From the moment a visitor passed through the gates of the ramparts, their path took them along a central axis to the centre of the city:

the forum. A network of parallel and perpendicular streets organised the rest of the space. Walls opposite private residences and public monuments were without windows, with the exception of the shops or *tabernae* on either side of most private residences. This, plus the absence of avenues (*plateae*) and city squares, made for a highly confined space. The only open square was the *forum*, and in reality, even this was not the case. Under Augustus, a new type of square was developed: the bloc-*forum*, tripartite and inaccessible to the general public (contrary to the *agora* of the first Greek cities or the original *forum* of Rome). Over time, access became more tightly controlled, and as a result, the main streets ended up bypassing the *forum*. When this happened, the *forum*'s location shifted away from its once-central location. The absence of avenues or squares likely conditioned the location of certain buildings related to entertainment, especially when their construction occurred much later after the city's foundation.

Through the streets passed all manner of raw materials, brought in from the surrounding territory and from trade, which were then either transformed by artisans or else used in their raw state (e.g., firewood, building materials, and foodstuffs). The city itself served as a centre of redistribution for the region and nearby settlements. Commercial, artisanal, and residential spaces coexisted. Of course, as noted by A. Wallace-Hadrill, commercial and artisanal activities tended to be concentrated in the most important streets, such as in *Herculaneum* or, as we saw, *Durocortorum* (Reims).

Vitruvius devotes an entire chapter (*De Architectura*, I, 6) to the urban grid and the distribution of streets both wide (*platea*) and narrow (*agriportus*). His account, however, does not correspond to the dominant manner of urban planning of his time, which made no differentiation between the two. Instead, their distribution was designed to prevent prevailing winds from blowing through the streets. Vitruvius says nothing of sewers. However, archaeological discoveries, as in *Augusta Praetoria* (Aosta, Italy), demonstrate that these underground networks reproduced almost exactly the layout of the streets, and therefore must have preceded them.

The *Lex Ursonensis*, named after the *Colonia Iulia Genetiva* (Urso, Spain), regulated the flow of traffic. It reinforced the public nature of roadways, paths, and trails, as well as the principles that served to preserve private interests – even in cases where a *duumvir* technically oversaw the *vias, fossas,* and *cloacas*, as noted by archeologists working in far-flung Roman territories such as northern Gaul. Their responsibilities included ensuring roadways were level, constructing gutters, and laying down gravel (city streets were not always paved, contrary to what the roadways of Pompeii and Herculaneum may suggest). Porticos, sidewalks, and other such elements were often maintained at the behest of civic authorities and residents, with an eye towards maintaining straight architectural lines. In colder regions, porticos allowed for foot traffic in all types of weather and could be found in capitals and smaller settlements alike.

4 The Domus and Family Unit

The *domus* was the residence of the *pater familias*, his family and household. This included the master, the *pater familias*, the extended family up to three generations, and slaves. In other words, a unit both familial and productive in nature, from the highest (the *dominus*) to the lowest (the *servus*) on the social scale.

The overall layout of the Roman house appears to have been more or less stable through time. However, certain evolutions from the end of the Republic and the Augustan era nonetheless reflect changes in Roman society. As demonstrated by P. Gros, no real comparison can be drawn between the spatial organisation of the domestic residence and that of the city. Any such comparison is more a matter of allusion than actual 'proportional homothety', reminiscent of the connection drawn by Aristotle between home and *civitas*. A metaphorical comparison, therefore, in much the same way the meaning of the word *imperium* (initially the 'public power of the magistrate') was transferred onto 'the domestic power of the *pater familias*' – a comparison which allowed ancient authors to make references between the *civitas* and the *domus*. For the ancients, the *domus* was organised around areas of reception and representation. The *loca communia* were freely accessible. Spaces of worship (the *lararium*); spaces for strolling (the *peristylium*); decorated, plastered galleries with painted landscapes; and gardens with fountains, such as the *hortus*, were all spaces with restricted access. The whole ensemble was proportioned according to the principles of Vitruvian architecture.

As noted by A. Wallace-Hadrill, members of the different social strata of the *clientele* (slaves, freedmen, clients, etc.) were housed in the *domus*, without separate spaces according to sex or age. The only difference was that of status. The goal of domestic Roman architecture was to provide the domestic unit with the appropriate spaces and contexts to organise the various activities that took place there. This is why, contrary to cities of other periods, the Roman urban space knew no social segregation, with the exception of the *insulae* and certain sectors of the *Urbs* and, in all likelihood, other large cities.

Beyond this, as suggested by the work of P. Gros, a social transformation was undeniably at work between the end of the Republic and the start of the principate which had an impact on the urban *domus* and promoted different spatial and ornamental solutions. Hellenistic influences can be seen at all levels of artistic and material production. This Hellenisation, evident even in Roman names, brought new social codes and architectural formulations designed to 'fully articulate the *maiestas*', in accordance with styles of public architecture imported from the East. Such transformations in Rome and Italy were the object of much discussion between supporters of tradition and innovation. In the later-Romanised, western provinces, on the other hand, they became the new archetype of Roman architecture.

Note

1 That is, groupings of monuments spatially related to one another through contiguity, alignment, and perspective.

Bibliography

Andreau, J., L'espace de la vie financière à Rome, in *L'Urbs: Espace urbain et histoire (Ier siècle av. J.-C. – IIIe siècle ap. J.-C.). Actes du colloque international de Rome (8–12 mai 1985), École Française de Rome*, Roma, École française de Rome, 1987, pp. 157–174.

Arce, J., Goffaux, B. (dirs.), *Horrea d'Hispanie et de la Méditerranée romaine*, Madrid, Casa de Velázquez, 2011.

Ballet, P., Dieudonné-Glad, N., Saliou, C. (dirs.), *La Rue dans l'Antiquité. Définition, aménagement et devenir de l'Orient méditerranéen à la Gaule*, Rennes, Presses Universitaires de Rennes, 2008.

Cleary, S. E., Public Buildings in the Cities of Roman Britain: Successes or Failures? in L. Brassous, A. Quevedo Sánchez (dirs.), *Urbanisme civique en temps de crise. Les espaces publics d'Hispanie et de l'Occident romain entre le IIe et le IVe siècle*, Madrid, Casa de Velazquez, 2015, pp. 63–82.

Cousins, E. H., *The Sanctuary at Bath in the Roman Empire*, Cambridge, Cambridge University Press, 2020.

Cristilli, A., *Macellum* and *Imperium*. The Relationship Between the Roman State and the Market-Building Construction, *Analysis Archaeologica an International Journal of Western Mediterranean Archaeology*, 1, 2015, pp. 69–86.

Davenport, P., *Roman Bath: A New History and Archaeology of Aquae Sulis*, Gloucestershire, The History Press, 2021.
Dechezleprêtre, T., Gruel, K., Joly, M. (dir.), *Agglomérations et sanctuaires. Réflexions à partir de l'exemple de Grand, Actes du colloque de Grand, 20–23 octobre 2011*, Épinal, Conseil Départemental des Vosges, 2015.
De Ruyt, C., *Macellum, marché alimentaire des Romains*, Louvain-la-Neuve, Institut Supérieur D'archéologie et D'histoire de L'art, 1983.
Dumasy, F., Théâtres et amphithéâtres dans les cités de Gaule Romaine: Fonctions et répartition, *Études de lettres*, 1(2), 2011, pp. 193–222.
Flohr, M., Commerce and Architecture in Late Hellenistic Italy: The Emergence of the Taberna Row, in M. Flohr, N. Monteix (eds.), *Shops, Workshops and Urban Economic History in the Roman World. Proceedings of the 19th International Congress of Classical Archaeology*, Heidelberg, Propylaeum, 2020, pp. 1–11.
García Garrido, M., Mangas Manjarrés, J., La Lex Ursonensis: Estudio y edición crítica, *Studia historica. Historia Antigua*, 15, Salamanca, Universidad de Salamanca, 1997.
Grimal, P., *Les villes Romaines*, Paris, Presses Universitaires de France, 1954 = *Roman cities*, Madison, University of Wisconsin Press, 1983.
Gros, P., La ville comme symbole. Le modèle central et ses limites, in H. Inglebert (dir.), *Histoire de la civilisation Romaine*, Paris, Presses Universitaires de France, 2005, pp. 155–232.
Gros, P., La maison romaine selon Vitruve: Statut du texte et stratification de l'exposé, *Scholion*, 10, 2016, pp. 65–90.
Gros, P., Torelli, M., *Storia dell'Urbanistica. Il mondo romano*, 1st edition, Roma – Bari, Laterza, 1988–2007.
Kenyon, K., The Roman Theatre at Verulamium, *Archaeologia*, 84, 1935, pp. 213–261.
Nelis-Clément, J., Roddaz, J. M. (eds.), *Le cirque romain et son image*, Bordeaux, Ausonius, 2008.
Ney, C., Didierjean, F., Paillet, J. L., *Belo III. Le Macellum*, Madrid, Casa de Velázquez, 1986.
Perring, D., Spatial Organisation and Social Change in Roman Towns, in J. Rich, A. Wallace-Hadrill (eds.), *City and Country in the Ancient World*, New York, Routledge, 1991, pp. 273–293.
Tillier, C., Armirotti, A., González Villaescusa, R., Eaux souterraines et eaux superficielles: de la fondation d'Augusta Prætoria à la Aoste médiévale (Italie), in E. Lorans, T. Pouyet et G. Simon (dirs.), *L'eau dans les villes d'Europe au Moyen Âge (IVe–XVe siècle)*, RACF, Tours, 2023, pp. 239–253.
Wallace-Hadrill, A., *Houses and Households of Pompeii. Houses and Society in Pompeii and Herculaneum*, Princeton, Princeton University Press, 1994.

7 Life and Death in the City

1 Urban Density and Demographics

Initial estimates place the historical population of the Roman Empire at around 54 million inhabitants at the death of Augustus and at 70 million by the middle of the 2nd century AD. For our purposes, it is primarily the growth of the population and the density of cities and towns that are of interest, by virtue of their impact on the Roman urban network.

The number of cities in the empire is estimated to have been between 2,000 and 2,700, each having a population of around 20,000 to 26,000 inhabitants, of which 2,000 to 6,000 resided – or at least had a residence – within the ramparts. With the exception of the large megalopolises of antiquity with more than 100,000 inhabitants, which were rare, the urban population was small, and the majority of cities would have been, in our eyes, rather modest settlements.

Overall, the population of a *civitas* would have been fairly evenly distributed across its territory. The larger it was, the greater the number of settlements it would have contained. That said, regions more densely studded with *civitates* were necessarily more populous, and so the density was proportional. Smaller settlements were even more regularly distributed than *civitates*, which were subject to greater irregularity.

Traditionally, high birth and death rates in cities have translated into an overall negative population balance: more inhabitants die than are born, as in Paris in the 17th century. And yet, despite the higher mortality rates than in rural areas, the Empire's urban population grew exponentially. According to W. Scheidel, the period in question was part of a global trend of population growth between the end of the Bronze Age and the modern era, with the rate of natural increase rising by 0.1% per year. This rise in the urban population can only be explained by a rural exodus. According to Scheidel, Roman cities were charged with absorbing the surplus of the natural rural population growth that would otherwise have led to an overpopulation of the countryside (an argument much discussed by authors like E. Lo Cascio and B. Friers). This model implies a kind of 'zero-sum game' between the populations of the countryside and the city, such that the overall rate of population growth was minor.

And yet, migratory movement from the countryside to the city seems to have been relatively small, as demonstrated by C. Moatti. A far call, anyway, from the great rural exodus of the Industrial Revolution. It's important to remember that freedom of movement was not at all guaranteed in the empire, even for free men, who were invariably governed by the rules of patronage (whether they were free from birth or had been emancipated). The only reference likely to provide an answer to this thorny question comes from a 2nd-century text, the *Papyrus Giessen* (40, III-IV). It transcribes an edict of expulsion from the city of Alexandria, where the interests of peasants were wholly disregarded in favour of more worthy public causes – namely 'pig merchants, boatmen, and those who bring reeds to heat the baths'. Another group of urban traders, linen weavers, is held in opposition to 'rural Egyptians' (*agroíkous aiguptioús*), judged incapable of adopting an 'urban behaviour' (*anastrophês [po]leitikês*). In other words, farmers – the labour force of large landowners and an important source of tax revenues for small estates – were not expected to move to the city, even if the evidence of such a text, supported by estimates of rural-to-urban migration figures, testifies to the fact that they did. If Scheidel's calculations are correct, the 40 million inhabitants who would have migrated to the city over the course of a millennium would only represent about 20 people per year and per city. Even if one exaggerates these estimates by 10 or even 100, the phenomenon would still have been far from problematic and rather proves that the demographic growth of Roman cities was quite modest during the first three centuries AD. No doubt, in every region, urban migration was a consequence of the proliferation of urban settlements, especially in the less urbanised regions that Rome encountered during its expansion. Apart from the great megalopolises, however, and the main regional urban centres, archaeology has been unable to demonstrate that cities created during the period in question grew significantly in surface area.

Excluding the significant migratory movements recorded by the available data (and disregarding the deportations and displacements of subjugated populations), how can we explain the arrival of new inhabitants in the empire's cities? Research has historically emphasised the role that the agrarian crises of the end of the Republic must have played, dispossessing small and medium-sized landowners of their estates and thus bolstering the cities' working classes. But, as we have seen, this cannot fully account for the overall growth in population. Unless, of course, one accepts a rate of growth of around 0.2%, in line with the more expansive models, which could then explain both the Empire's overall population growth and a continuous flow of rural populations into the city, offsetting the higher urban mortality rates.

2 Pathologies and Illness in the City

The history of urbanism and its diffusion is also the history of infectious diseases. Some of them, such as poliomyelitis or smallpox, are closely tied to the urban development of certain regions: Mesopotamia, ancient Egypt, the Indus Valley, and the first Chinese cities. Overcrowding and other factors that facilitate the communication of disease favoured the emergence of new viruses and variants. The city was subject to its own set of demographic and pathological dynamics.

While the achievements of Roman cities in terms of 'macroscopic hygiene' were not insignificant (e.g., water supply, sewers, public baths, and latrines), it was not until the 20th century that the West discovered 'microscopic hygiene'. A. Scobie has shown how overcrowding and the lack of modern medical knowledge in Antiquity greatly facilitated the transmission of infectious agents. Despite the existence of aqueducts, it was also impossible to control water purity at a microscopic level, and contaminations could occur at multiple points in the water cycle. An average city of 20,000 inhabitants produced up to 10 tons of human waste. Sewers served as drainage networks, but wastewater was not separated from rainwater. In addition, private households lacked the plumbing necessary to prevent waste from resurfacing, especially in the case of blockages or during periods of river flooding. Thermal baths were frequented by the sick as well as the healthy, at least until the time of Emperor Hadrian, who enforced their separation. In short, the conditions were very much like those of preindustrial cities where life expectancy at birth was between 25 and 30 years, and between 35 and 37 years for individuals who survived their first 10 years of life.

Many diseases arrived in a region with the first Roman cities, spreading to newly conquered, previously non-urbanised zones. Despite the level of uncertainty that necessarily accompanies this kind of data,

C. Roberts and M. Cox have identified the presence of typically urban pathogens in Roman Brittany, the most recently conquered region of the West, which is incontrovertible proof – if any were needed – of the relationship between these pathologies and the island's invasion at the time of Emperor Claudius. Among the infectious diseases that most often struck cities were poliomyelitis, tuberculosis, meningitis, and leprosy. Other diseases affecting the wealthier social classes, such as gout, were the result of distinctly 'urban', protein-rich diets. Finally, comparing archaeological data from urban and rural necropolises has made it possible to identify major incidences of certain diseases, such as infantile tuberculosis.

Medical care seems to have been mostly a private affair. Practitioners and the medical sciences were often of Greek origin. Sanctuaries of healing deities such as Apollo and his son, Aesculapius (whose statues often graced the baths), served as spaces of public health. The Greek god Asclepius took on the role of healer in Rome under his Latinised name from the start of the 3rd century BC and in all the Empire's conquered territories up until the Byzantine era. Medical science was practised in *asclépiéia* – sanctuaries transformed in the earliest days of the Roman Empire into hospitals and teaching centres. Professional guilds or *collegia* provided a social framework for their members and played a fundamental role in public health and the treatment of ailments.

Deserving of special mention are public physicians, who practised in Greece and, like grammarians and professors of rhetoric, were hired by the *Curia* of certain Western cities. They enjoyed political immunity and other privileges accorded by the State, especially during the 2nd century, as well as increased remuneration from the 3rd century AD. In the West, *P. Frontinius Siscola, medicus colonorum coloniae Patriciae* (Cordoba), was one such physician. Elsewhere, with the exception of military camps on the Rhine or in Brittany, practitioners operated mainly in cities (in the capitals of provinces and *civitates* and various other settlements). Indeed, few epitaphs have been found in the countryside.

Although he lived beyond the chronological and geographical contexts of the present work, Basil of Caesarea is known for having founded the first hospice intended to accommodate the old, the poor, and the sick in his native city during the 4th century AD (and thus well before the first urban mediaeval medical institutions). Veritable 'miniature towns', as remarked by Gregory of Nazianzus, these '*basiliades*' were the answer to a problem that, although it had arisen long before the end of the Roman era, helped establish a new type of society in which the Church replaced the independents and professional guilds of the classical era in matters of public health.

3 Waste and Excrement

Lead pipes, used abundantly in the Roman Empire, were thought to be the cause of lead pollution and lead poisoning epidemics. This thesis was effectively disproven by H. Delile, though, whose research shows that, despite the quantities of lead found in the waters of the Tiber and the basin of Trajan's harbour, which are certainly excessive by today's standards, these waters 'were not sufficiently rich in lead to have constituted a major health risk'. Nonetheless, lead contamination is a reliable marker of socioeconomic conditions. High levels of lead have been found in the sediments of the High Roman Empire and in the dental enamel of skeletons unearthed from the same area. A drop in the sedimentary level of lead as early as the 3rd century AD reveals a malfunction in the poorly maintained plumbing system of Rome. Finally, the reappearance of sedimentary lead as early as the 6th century may be related to the reopening of this system in the Byzantine era.

More important, but less obvious, was the contamination caused by poor air quality inside houses and in the streets. Charcoal particles and other toxic elements related to combustion, produced by oil lamps, stoves, the heating of households and baths, and artisanal activities using fire, undoubtedly had a significant impact on the health of the citizens of all cities, especially where respiratory diseases are concerned. The thoraces of skeletons found at *Herculaneum* show traces of visceral lesions, a sign of pleural inflammation due to anthracosis.

The archaeological record shows the effects of urban waste management and landfills (or rather, the lack thereof). In general, waste production in pre-industrial cities was quite different from what it is today. 'Recycling' was more common, for one. Like today, the household waste of antiquity was composed of vegetal waste, bones with scraps of meat on them, fruit pits, and other culinary waste (*stercus*). But lacking any modern notion of waste sorting, the Ancients simply disposed of waste all mixed together. Today, these ancient dumps, where fragments of *amphorae*, broken crockery, and organic matter can be found, are a boon for archaeologists. While organic remains have mostly disappeared, pottery and bones remain, and their study has allowed us to deepen our understanding of Roman society, both culturally and chronologically as well as anthropologically and economically. Especially interesting is the relation that existed between these dumps and the inhabitants and governance of the city. For example, their location is fundamental to understanding how they were managed and how the attitudes of urban populations evolved.

For simplicity's sake, let us distinguish between two categories of waste sites. First, those that formed spontaneously, in close proximity to spaces where waste was produced, such as at the corner of a house, in a little-frequented dead-end of the city, or to fill in an existing hole. These were managed privately. Likewise, certain areas were kept clean on the impetus of private citizens, such as when a street was maintained by its residents, just as they sometimes built sidewalks or porticos. Dumps of this type were smaller and appeared spontaneously; the main concern was that they be hidden from view. Slightly larger dumps are associated with ports and the voluntary unloading or accidental loss of materials, as demonstrated by archaeological discoveries made under the waters of the Rhône or in the ancient ports of Marseilles and Arles.

Second, public dumps (sometimes privately managed, like the *stercorarii* in Rome) served the purpose of removing waste from the city. For this reason, the remains of such dumps are typically found beyond the city walls, forming large-scale archaeological deposits. Here could be found waste collected through street cleaning, organised by city authorities. An important and unique example of this style of waste management is Mount Testaccio in Rome, an artificial hill 35 metres high. It is the result of the accumulation of shards (*testae*) of millions of *amphorae* from all over the empire – a little more than half a cubic hectometre of rubble, most of which was the result of shipping activity along the Tiber and from the warehouses of the *horrea Aemilia*.

Dumps of the first type are notably associated with the earliest phases of a city's existence, as can be seen in *Lugdunum* (Lyon). But as soon as urban authorities began to improve road and sewage systems and as the quality of life improved, dumps seem to have been organised in a collective, even public manner and began appearing outside of cities throughout the High Empire. In Late Antiquity, cities saw the appearance of vacant and abandoned lots (as a consequence of poor upkeep), which stimulated the formation of small, spontaneous dumps within the city. The phenomenon appeared and reappeared in *Lugdunum* all throughout the Empire's life and varied from city to city. It has been observed in *Carthago Nova* (Cartagena, Spain) from the 2nd century onward; in *Augustudunum* (Autun) towards the 4th century AD; and in *Tarraco* (Tarragona, Spain) from the 5th century AD. Sewage systems underwent a similar change. A general lack of maintenance coincided with clogging from sediments found in surface waters and the presence of waste. Once again, local histories offer a variety of dates, ranging from the middle of the 3rd century for *Augusta Praetoria* (Aosta, Italy) and Lyon to the 3rd and 4th centuries for certain Hispanic sites. Renewed use of the sewer system of Ravenna in the 5th and 6th centuries, no doubt due to the revitalisation of port and urban activity during this period, demonstrates the connection between this infrastructure and urban life.

4 Death and the City

As previously mentioned (see Chapter 4), funeral pyres in Rome were not allowed within 500 paces (736 metres) of the *pomœrium*. Beyond this could be found necropolises and spaces for *ustrina* or cremations. Arguments related to hygiene are often cited to explain this remoteness, mirroring the 'biopolitical' concerns of modern city planning. But A. Scobie has demonstrated how not only animal but also human corpses frequently littered the streets of Rome or were thrown into the sewers, despite the strict prescriptions of law and custom. Therefore, one can only agree with N. Laubry when he places legal and administrative considerations on the same level as fears of infection. The proscription of leaving the dead within the city limits was intended to prevent their burial (*funus*) within private spaces. Similarly, in his commentary on the Law of the Twelve Tablets, Cicero justifies the ban on funeral pyres by risk of fire.

The location of necropolises thus draws a fundamental topographical boundary, making it possible to better understand the total extent of the urban space. In the rural territory of the city, the burial site, as a lasting space dedicated to lesser gods, a '*locus religiosus*', served as a boundary marker for ancient surveyors (*De Sepulchris*, Lachmann 271, 20). Similarly, sacred spaces on the borders of territories, like mausoleums and temples, often dedicated to Mercury or to the *lares* of the *compitalia* (crossroads), helped to define city boundaries.

Like the *suburbia*, urban necropolises were placed in a circle around the ramparts and along the roads that connected the city to its territory and the wider world. Their organisation into distinct zones or *areae* (mausoleums, funerary enclosures, and more humble burials), visible to visitors and those who made the daily commute between the town and countryside, was a reflection of the society's various social strata. As in the *domus*, the different generations of *patres familias* shared funerary spaces, and the quality and grandeur of their funeral monuments, from imposing mausoleums to collective and individual burial sites clad in tiles, served as a demonstration of social position. Necropolises thus serve as a record of a city's past social configurations and, of course, the great families that governed them.

The city's elites had the choice between being buried near the city or else *in suo fundo*, that is, on their rural property, provided it was situated at a certain distance from residential spaces. J.-L. Fiches has shown how the burials, *cippi*, inscriptions, and mausoleums of the *civitas* of Nîmes tended to be concentrated in agricultural zones owned by local landed elites whose wealth grew after the arrival of the Romans.

Bibliography

Alonso, M. A., Los *medici* en la epigrafía de la Hispania romana, *Veleia*, 28, 2011, pp. 83–107.

Armirotti, A., Joris, C., Lo scavo delle cantine di Casa Favre-Bagicalupi in via Croce di Città ad Aosta. Nuovi dati sulla topografia di Aosta Praetoria, *Bollettino della Soprintendenza per i beni e le attività culturali*, 10, 2013, pp. 38–44.

Ballet, P., Cordier, P., Dieudonné-Glad, N. (dirs.), *La Ville et ses déchets dans le monde romain: Rebuts et recyclages. Actes du colloque de Poitiers (19–21 septembre 2002)*, Montagnac, Éditions Mergoil, 2003.

Capasso, L., Indoor pollution and respiratory diseases in Ancient Rome, *The Lancet*, 256, 2000, p. 1774.

Delile, H., Les paléo-pollutions au plomb, témoins des conditions socio-économiques de la Rome antique, *Médecine/sciences, EDP Sciences*, 30(10), 2014, pp. 831–833.

Delile, H., Blichert-Toft, J., Goirand, J. P., Keay, S., Albarède, F., Lead in ancient Rome's city waters, *PNAS*, 111(18), 2014, pp. 6594–6599.

Dupré-Raventos, X., Remolà, J. A., Sordes urbis. *La eliminación de residuos en la ciudad romana. Actas de la reunión de Roma (15-16 de noviembre de 1996)*, Roma, L'Erma di Bretschneider, 2000.

Fiches, J. L., Les élites nîmoises et les campagnes au Haut-Empire: Caractérisation, place et signification de leurs sépultures, in *Monde des morts, monde des vivants en Gaule rurale, Actes du Colloque ARCHEA/AGER (Orléans, 7–9 février 1992)*, Tours, Fédération pour l'édition de la Revue archéologique du Centre de la France, 1993, pp. 333–339.

Frier, B. W., More Is Worse: Some Observations on the Population of the Roman Empire, in W. Scheidel (dir.), *Debating Roman Demography*, Leyde – Boston, Brill, 2001, pp. 139–159.

Havlíček, F., Morcinek, M., Waste and Pollution in the Ancient Roman Empire, *Journal of Landscape Ecology*, 9(3), 2016, pp. 33–49.

Hope, V. M., Marshall, E. (eds.), *Death and Disease in the Ancient City*, London – New York, Routledge, 2000.

Jongman, W. M., Jacobs, J. P. A. M., Goldewijk, G. M. K., Health and Wealth in the Roman Empire, *Economics and Human Biology*, 34, 2019, pp. 138–150.

Laubry, N., Le transfert des corps dans l'Empire romain: Problèmes d'épigraphie, de religion et de droit romain, *Mélanges de l'École française de Rome. Antiquité*, 119(1), 2007, pp. 149–188.

Lebret, J. B., Agusta-Boularot, S. (dirs.), Dossier: La gestion des eaux indésirables dans le monde romain, *Revue archéologique de Narbonnaise*, 2022, pp. 54–55.

Lo Cascio, E., The Size of the Roman Population: Beloch and the Meaning of the Augustan Census Figures, *The Journal of Roman Studies*, 84, 1994, pp. 23–40.

Remolà, J. A., Acero-Pérez J. (dirs.), *La Gestión de los residuos urbanos en Hispania. Xavier Dupré Raventós (1956–2006), in memoriam*, Mérida, CSIC, 2011.

Rémy, B., Faure, P., *Les médecins dans l'Occident romain*, Nouvelle édition, Pessac, Ausonius Éditions, 2010.

Rodríguez-Neila, J. F., *Medicus Colonorum. Los médicos oficiales de las ciudades en época romana*, Córdoba, Universidad de Córdoba, 1977.

Scheidel, W., Demography, in Scheidel, W, Morris, I., Saller, R. (eds.), *The Cambridge Economic History of the Greco-Roman World*, Cambridge, Cambridge University Press, 2007, pp. 38–86.

Scheidel, W., Disease and Death in the Ancient City of Rome, *Princeton/Stanford Working Papers in Classics*, 2009 [Online: http://dx.doi.org/10.2139/ssrn.1347510].

Scobie, A., Slums, Sanitation, and Mortality in the Roman World, *Klio*, 68–2, 1986, pp. 399–433.

Tilburg, C. V., *Streets and Streams: Health Conditions and City Planning in the Graeco-Roman World*, Leiden, Primavera Pers, 2015.

Epilogue
The End of the *Civitas*

A relatively modest *civitas* located in the region of Latium, Rome was able to extend its territory and rule by consolidating a vast array of scattered and dissimilar cities and peoples – a process that was not complete until the beginning of the 3rd century BC, when a single civic status was finally established for all free men and conquered territories. The incorporation of such a diverse set of peoples and regions was a slow-paced phenomenon. As more cities and towns were founded, the empire's urban network became more dense. At the same time, channels of communication and transportation (streets, roads, stopovers, waterways and artificial canals, and ports) further developed to facilitate the movement of peoples, goods, and information. The resulting network varied in density according to the existing infrastructure it encountered: closer-knit where urban centres were most dense before the arrival of the Romans and sparser in more distant regions, where outposts were preferred.

Civitates were the basic units of this network. In some cases, they were superimposed upon a pre-existing town; in others, they were created *ex nihilo* and a population made to assemble within a central urban settlement whose surrounding territory, by virtue of its diverse landscape, ensured their subsistence. These cities served many functions, including as political, cultural, spatial, and fiscal extensions of Rome – a fact well demonstrated by their characteristically monumental architecture. But this practice, and the defence of such a vast territory, was costly in energy and resources.

The city of Rome was modelled after the *polis*; an epigone of the *ideal-type* of the city-state that had appeared a thousand years earlier. The *civitates* of the Empire enjoyed a limited form of internal autonomy at the end of the Roman Republic and the beginning of the principate, as lamented by Plutarch (*Precepts of Statecraft*, 805 a-b). But this ended with the reforms of Diocletian and the emergence of the Tetrarchy at the end of the 3rd century and beginning of the 4th century AD. *Civitates* and major cities started to disappear or else underwent profound transformations. In the East, however, where urban expansion had first begun, demographic and economic conditions continued to favour the survival of *civitates*. In fact, certain characteristics of these city-states persisted into the 6th century. Here, the *civitas* and its particular form of urban life endured as they had during the High Empire.

The gradual transformation of *civitates* and urban culture was evidence of a major social change, reflected in the very spatial nature of the Empire, starting with the transfer of its capital to the East: the refoundation of Constantinople in 330 AD, undertaken according to the architectural methods of the previous era (though, of course, Constantinople underwent important transformations relatively soon thereafter, as demonstrated by the presence of new forms of monumentalism).

Organicism serves as a useful metaphor here. The model of the *civitas* and its corollary, the ancient city, were the result of a market economy and long-distance trade: *civitates* and cities formed a network connecting the various cells of the empire, whose energy requirements continued to grow. The more advanced the urban world became, the greater its level of interconnectedness and the more interdependent its inhabitants became. As B. Frier reminds us, demographic variables are essential to economic reasoning. Beyond its capacity for predation – and as a direct consequence of it – the Roman Empire owed its wealth to the enormous size of its population and, of course, its capacity to transform the environment to suit its needs. For example, the Empire's defensive model reached a kind of threshold under Tiberius, where its effectiveness was mostly a function of the sheer number of soldiers, whose presence alone was a powerful deterrent to resistance. There's little doubt this model served as a factor of dynamism for the regions within the Empire's borders. But it required an expenditure of energy that far outstripped initial investments. The 40,000 legionnaires along the Rhenish *limes* were costly indeed. A state must invariably provide for those parts of its population that do not produce what they consume. To this was added the costs of infrastructure (building materials and maintenance), which grew as urban, transport, and defence installations became more numerous, in an ever-expanding effort to reach every corner of the Empire. The Empire's cities, which consumed the vast majority of the resources produced in the surrounding rural territories, were both a symbol of and the physical manifestation of this system.

But after the Empire began syphoning money from the cities in favour of a more direct style of fiscal management in the 4th century AD, trust between Rome and the cities' local elites quickly eroded. The need arose to focus on defensive infrastructure, resulting in the construction of new ramparts and other territorial defence systems. As a result, interactions between regional urban elites and the heart of the empire were greatly reduced, and all the energy initially reserved for promoting and maintaining the model of the *civitas* was gradually repurposed.

The consequences of this transformation are especially visible in the changing urban infrastructure of the time. The vast majority of aqueducts, for example, ceased to function after the 3rd century. The aqueduct of Nîmes is a particularly telling example. A lack of regular cleaning and maintenance, especially of the pipes, led the inhabitants of the surrounding countryside to divert the water for their own uses from the middle of the 3rd century onwards. Thus, the city's enormous initial investment eventually led to returns for other, more rural populations. Likewise, the entire system of drainage of the colony of *Augusta Praetoria* (Aosta, Italy) appears to have been defunct by as early as the Flavian dynasty, and the colony's large sewers were blocked in places as early as the end of the 3rd century. From the 6th century onwards, the inhabitants of the city instead relied on a surface network for the supply and evacuation of water from the Aosta Valley.

Certain cities, such as *Carthago Nova* (Cartagena, Spain), whose lucrative mines had attracted the attention of republican Rome, soon proved unable to maintain their public buildings. Both the importance and productivity of public offices declined as the city was deprived of resources to ever greater extents. Such signs of decline can be seen in a majority of cities from the following century onward. The grand and majestic buildings created to house city spectacles, baths, theatres, amphitheatres, and circuses fell into disrepair as the impetus for euergetism waned. In the 4th and 5th centuries, only rarely are such buildings and infrastructure maintained; more often, they are repurposed for housing or raw materials. Ruins abound, and abandoned houses and buildings are converted into local dumps. Streets are progressively privatised by residents. The manufacture of goods, on the other hand, did not disappear from urban settings: glass and metal workshops, for example, took root in abandoned spaces.

Agricultural production followed much the same evolution, with rural settlements undergoing an important reorganisation. The clearing and exploitation of land and the reclamation of swamplands reached its peak during the 2nd century AD. From this point on, agricultural output started to decline. The appearance of so-called 'opportunistic'[1] farming appeared as early as the 1st century AD, but soon disappeared from the countryside; as early as the 2nd century in some regions, as late as the 3rd or 4th in others. The archaeological record demonstrates a paradoxical relationship between the depopulation of the countryside on the one hand, and a certain rebirth of late antique rural residences on the other, owing to the fact that investments from the landed elite, once funnelled into the city, were now being used to embellish and improve their own rural residences as a display of wealth. Thus, resources previously sent to the city were diverted to the countryside.

Paleo-environmental and landscape archaeology has shown that, as lands conquered during the great expansion were abandoned and investments in their maintenance dropped off, many regions experienced reforestation and the expansion of wetlands. From the Iron Age and through the Gallo-Roman period, and from the Rhone Valley to the coastal plains of Lower Normandy, we see evidence of developing irrigation networks and the draining of wetlands for agropastoral production. At the end of Antiquity, though, the abandonment of these systems led to the return of wetlands and the proliferation of trees and shrubs on valley floors as well as an increase in agropastoral activity, often associated with these new forests and meadows.

Like the 'opportunistic' farmlands mentioned here, all the settlements created by the Empire to flesh out its urban network no longer had any reason to exist, and many of them disappeared. The last remaining regions and peoples hitherto denied citizenship were afforded this privilege with the Edict of Caracalla in 212 AD. Thereafter, between the 4th and 6th centuries, a meagre hundred or so cities were founded or promoted.

From the 3rd century onwards, the economic and political situation recovered, but on new footing. The general economic growth of the 4th century, and the increase in population and the prosperity of certain regions in Africa and the East, allowed some cities of the West to maintain their existence, thanks to their geographic or political proximity to these regions. But many other cities disappeared. Some of those that survived and even thrived did so thanks to this new geopolitical context and the arrival of the Germanic people, undertaking novel functions and configurations.

The system of the *civitates*, which reached its peak while the Roman Empire was at peace, had succeeded in extending citizenship and the urban way of life to areas previously denied them. Rome's interests at this time extended to the far reaches of the known world: Cadiz, located at the Strait of Gibraltar, for example. The Vicarello Cups show that it was possible to travel from Rome to Cadiz in one continuous journey, following the Mediterranean coast (even if, of course, the network of routes and relays varied in density along the way). Travellers who crossed the great urban gap between Sagonte and *Dertosa*, for example, found only *stationes* here, as it remained devoid of cities throughout Antiquity.

The network of *civitates*, their cities and territories, began to thin, especially in regions where it had been less dense to begin with or where they failed to find new social, economic, or political functions. This is partly what differentiated it from the East. Indeed, the civic and urban structures of the West were much more recent, and the Roman *civitas* could only find purchase and proliferate in these spaces, where the social structures were so different, building upon and even replacing existing tribal structures.

Is it so surprising, given these conditions, that Brittany, located at the Western confines of Roman expansion, the furthest and last region to see the foundation of new Roman cities, was one of the very first, at the beginning of the 5th century, to sever its connections with Rome?

Note

1 At the height of the Empire (1st century and part of the 2nd century AD), the high demand for foodstuffs and the intense level of interconnectivity between different regions of the empire provoked the appearance of 'opportunistic' agricultural sites: small properties in marginal zones with very limited harvests. From the 2nd or 3rd century on, these are the first rural establishments to be abandoned.

Bibliography

Armirotti, A., Joris, C., Lo scavo delle cantine di Casa Favre-Bagicalupi in via Croce di Città ad Aosta. Nuovi dati sulla topografia di Aosta Praetoria, *Bollettino della Soprintendenza per i beni e le attività culturali*, 10, 2013, pp. 38–44.

Brassous, L., Quevedo Sánchez, A. (dirs.), *Urbanisme civique en temps de crise. Les espaces publics d'Hispanie et de l'Occident romain entre le IIe et le IVe siècle*, Madrid, Casa de Velazquez, 2015.

Fabre, G., Fiches, J. L., Paillet, J. L. (dir.), *L'aqueduc de Nîmes et le pont du Gard: Archéologie, géosystème, histoire*, 2nd edition, Paris, CNRS Éditions, 2000.

Frier, B. W., More Is Worse: Some Observations on the Population of the Roman Empire, in W. Scheidel (dir.), *Debating Roman Demography*, Leyde – Boston, Brill, 2001, pp. 139–159.

Quevedo Sánchez, A., Ramallo Sánchez, S. F., La dinámica evolutiva de Carthago Nova entre los siglos II y III, in L. Brassous, A. Quevedo Sánchez (dirs.), *Urbanisme civique en temps de crise. Les espaces publics d'Hispanie et de l'Occident romain entre le IIe et le IVe siècle*, Madrid, Casa de Velazquez, 2015, pp. 161–177.

Index

Modern place names

Alcántara (ESP) 53
Alcudia (de Pollença), *Pollentia* (ESP) 21
Alexandria, *Alexandria* (EGY) 1, 48, 79
Alise-Sainte-Reine, *Alesia* (FRA) 61
Amiens, *Samarobriua* (FRA) 33
Angers, *Iuliomagus* (FRA) 35
Antibes, *Antipolis* (FRA) 7, 21
Antioch, *Antiochia* (TUR) 48
Aosta, *Augusta Praetoria* (ITA) 37, 74, 84, 89
Apamea, *Apamea* (SYR) 48
Arles, *Arelate* (FRA) 37, 52, 70, 73, 83
Astorga, *Asturica Augusta* (ESP) 22
Athens, *Athenae* (GRE) 69
Augsburg, *Augusta Vindelicum* (GER) 73
Autun, *Augustodunum* (FRA) 35, 62, 84
Avenches, *Aventicum* (SUI) 70
Az Zawiyah (district), *Sabratha* (LBA) 47

Bath, *Aquae Sulis* (ENG) 14, 72
Bavay, *Bagacum* (FRA) 33, 45, 70
Béziers, *Baeterrae* (FRA) 25
Bliesbruck, city of *Mediomatrici, Diuodorum*, cf. Metz (FRA) 46
Bolonia, *Baelo Claudia* (ESP) 61
Bordeaux, *Burdigala* (FRA) 33
Boulogne, *Gesoriacum* (FRA) 27, 33
Braga, *Bracara Augusta* (POR) 22

Cádiz, *Gades* (ESP) 12, 20, 91
Caerwent, *Venta Silurum* (WAL) 70
Cartagena, *Carthago Noua* (ESP) 83, 89
Carthage, *Carthago* (TUN) 23, 24, 48–51, 73, 83, 89
Cassel, *Castellum Menapiorum* (FRA) 35
Chesterholm, *Vindolanda* (ENG) 56
Cimiez (district of Nice), *Cemenelum* (FRA) 34, 72
Colchester, *Camulodunum* (ENG) 28, 73
Cologne, *Colonia Claudia Ara Agrippinensium* (GER) 13, 27, 33, 35
Condeixa-a-Velha (municipality), *Conimbriga* (POR) 70
Córdoba, *Corduba* (ESP) 81
Corinth, *Corinthus* (GRE) 69
Coruña del Conde, *Clunia* (ESP) 70

Cosa, *Cosa* (ITA) 11
Cupra Marittima, *Cupra Maritima* (ITA) 1

Dénia, *Dianium* (ESP) 21
Djem, El, *Thysdrus* (TUN) 23

Elche, *Ilici* (ESP) 55
Empúries, *Emporion* (ESP) 20–21, 33, 52, 61
Ephesus, *Éphesos* (TUR) 48
Espejo, *Ucubi* (ESP) 60
Evora, *Ebora* (POR) 70

Faimingen, *Phoebiana* (GER) 14
Fréjus, *Forum Iulii* (FRA) 25

Grand, *Aquae Granni*, (city of Andesina) (FRA) 14, 71
Graufesenque, La (Aveyron), *Condatomagus* (FRA) 62
Guardamar del Segura (Alicante) (ESP) 21

Herculaneum, *Herculaneum* (ITA) 74–75, 82

Ibiza, *Ebusus* (ESP) 21
Izmir, *Smyrna* (TUR) 48

Katwijk aan Zee, *Lugdunum Batavorum* (NED) 27
Kayseri, Eskişehir, *Mazaca Caesarea* (TUR) 81
Kerkouane (TUN) 23
Khoms, *Leptis Magna* (LBA) 47, 64

Langres, *Andemantunnum* (FRA) 33, 35, 53
Leicester, *Ratae Corieltauorum* (ENG) 73
León, Puente Castro, *Legio, ad Legionem* (ESP) 56
Lillebonne, *Juliobona* (FRA) 47

Lisbon, *Olisipo* (POR) 33
Llíria, *Edeta* (ESP) 72
London, *Londinium* (ENG) 28–29, 60, 62, 70
Lugo, *Lucus Augusti* (ESP) 22
Luni, *Luna* (ITA) 11, 63
Lyon, *Lugdunum* (FRA) 13, 33, 70, 83, 84

Maastricht, *Mosae Traiectum* (BEL) 46
Málaga (province), *Munda* (ESP) 22
Marseille, *Massalia* (FRA) 11, 12, 20, 24, 52, 83
Meknes (prefecture), *Volubilis* (MAR) 61
Mérida, *Emerita Augusta* (ESP) 60
Metz, *Diuodurum Mediomatricorum* (FRA) 46
Minturno, *Liris* (ITA) 11
Monaco, *Portus Herculis Monoecus* (MON) 55
Montbazin, *Forum Domitii* (FRA) 25
Montejo de Tiermes, *Termes* (ESP) 70

Nantes, *Portus Namnetorum, Condeuincum* (FRA) 33, 56
Narbonne, *Narbo Martius* (FRA) 25, 33, 53
Neumagen, *Noviomagus*, city of *Treveri*, cf. Trier) (GER) 46
Nice, *Nikaïa* (FRA) 6–7, 21, 34, 72
Nîmes, *Nemausus* (FRA) 13, 36, 63, 70, 85, 89
Nizy-le-Comte, *Minatiacum* (city of *Remi*, cf. Reims) (FRA) 46

Orange, *Arausio* (FRA) 25, 38, 70
Orleans, *Cenabum* (FRA) 35
Ostia, *Ostia* (ITA) 1, 11, 61
Osuna, *Urso* (ESP) 74

Palma de Mallorca, *Palma* (ESP) 21
Paris, *Lutetia* (FRA) 72
Pergamon, *Pergamum* (TUR) 48
Petronell, Bad Deutsch-Altenburg, *Carnuntum* (AUT) 56
Pompeii, *Pompeii* (ITA) 47, 61, 75
Pozzuoli, *Puteoli* (ITA) 11

Ravenna, *Ravenna* (ITA) 84
Reims, *Durocortorum* (FRA) 46, 53, 59, 61–62, 70, 74
Rezé, *Portus Pictonum, Ratiatum* (FRA) 33
Rome, *Roma* (ITA) 1, 9, 19, 33, 45, 60, 68, 79, 87

Saelices, *Segobriga* (ESP) 55, 70
Sagunto, *Saguntum* (ESP) 73, 91
Saint-Bertrand-de-Comminges, *Lugdunum Convenae* (FRA) 25, 73
Saint-Quentin, *Augusta Viromanduorum* (FRA) 36
San Roque, *Carteia* (ESP) 61
Santa Pola, *Portus Ilicitanus* (ESP) 21, 55
Setif, *Sitifis* (ALG) 73
Silchester, *Caleua Atrebatum* (ENG) 70
Sousse, *Hadrumetum* (TUN) 23
Strasbourg, *Argentoratum* (FRA) 56

Tarragona, *Tarraco* (ESP) 13, 55, 63, 84
Terracina, *Colonia Anxurnas* (ITA) 11
Timgad, *Thamugadi* (ALG) 19
Tipaza, *Tipasa* (ALG) 61
Tongeren, *Atuatuca* (BEL) 33, 34, 46
Tortosa, *Dertosa* (ESP) 91
Toulouse, *Tolosa* (FRA) 33, 64
Tours, *Caesarodunum* (FRA) 35

Trier, *Augusta Treuerorum* (GER) 33, 34, 46, 55, 70, 72
Tyre, *Tyrus* (LBN) 20, 23

Valencia, *Valentia* (ESP) 21, 22
Var (department), *Forum Voconii* (FRA) 25
Vieil-Evreux, *Gisacum* (FRA) 14
Vienna, *Vienna* (FRA) 72
Ventimiglia, *Albintimilium* (ITA) 56
Voorburg, *Forum Hadriani* (NED) 52

Ancient place names

Albintimilium, Ventimiglia (ITA) 56
Alesia, Alise-Sainte-Reine (FRA) 61
Alexandria, Alexandria (EGY) 48, 79
Andemantunnum, Langres (FRA) 33, 35, 53
Antiochia, Antioch (TUR) 48
Antipolis, Antibes (FRA) 7, 21
Apamea, Apamea (SYR) 48
Aquae Granni, (city of *Andesina*), Grand (FRA) 14, 71
Aquae Sulis, Bath (ENG) 14, 72
Arausio, Orange (FRA) 25, 38, 70
Arelate, Arles (FRA) 37, 52, 70, 73, 83
Argentoratum, Strasbourg (FRA) 56
Asturica Augusta, Astorga (ESP) 22
Athenae, Athens (GRE) 69
Atuatuca, Tongeren (BEL) 33, 34
Augusta Praetoria, Aosta (ITA) 37, 74, 84, 89
Augusta Treuerorum, Trier (GER) 33, 34, 46, 55, 70, 72
Augusta Vindelicum, Augsburg (GER) 73

Augusta Viromanduorum,
  Saint-Quentin (FRA) 36
Augustodunum, Autun (FRA) 35,
  62, 84
Aventicum, Avenches (SUI) 70

Baelo Claudia, Bolonia (ESP) 61
Baeterrae, Béziers (FRA) 25
Bagacum, Bavay (FRA) 33, 45, 70
Bracara Augusta, Braga (POR) 22
Burdigala, Bordeaux (FRA) 33

Caesarodunum, Tours (FRA) 35
Caleua Atrebatum, Silchester
  (ENG) 70
Camulodunum, Colchester
  (ENG) 28, 73
Carnuntum, Petronell, Bad
  Deutsch-Altenburg (AUT) 56
Carteia, San Roque (ESP) 61
Carthago, Carthage (TUN) 23,
  24, 48–51, 73, 83, 89
Carthago Noua, Cartagena
  (ESP) 83, 89
Castellum Menapiorum, Cassel
  (FRA) 17, 35
Cemenelum, Cimiez (district of
  Nice) (FRA) 34, 72
Cenabum, Orleans (FRA) 35
Clunia, Coruña del Conde
  (ESP) 70
Colonia Anxurnas, Terracina
  (ITA) 11
*Colonia Claudia Ara
  Agrippinensium*, Cologne
  (GER) 13, 27, 33, 35, 73
Condatomagus, La Graufesenque
  (Aveyron) (FRA) 62
Conimbriga, Condeixa-a-Velha
  (municipality) (POR) 70
Corduba, Córdoba (ESP) 81
Corinthus, Corinth (GRE) 69
Cosa, Cosa (ITA) 11
Cupra Maritima, Cupra
  Marittima (ITA) 1

Dertosa, Tortosa (ESP) 91
Dianium, Dénia (ESP) 21
Diuodorum, Metz (FRA) 46
Durocortorum, Reims (FRA) 46,
  53, 59, 61, 62, 70, 74

Ebora, Evora (POR) 70
Ebusus, Ibiza (ESP), 21
Edeta, Llíria (ESP), 72
Emerita Augusta, Mérida
  (ESP) 60
Emporion, Empúries (ESP)
  20–21, 33, 52, 61
Éphesos, Ephesos (TUR) 48

Forum Domitii, Montbazin
  (FRA) 25
Forum Hadriani, Voorburg
  (NED) 52
Forum Iulii, Fréjus (FRA) 25
Forum Voconii, Var (department)
  (FRA) 25

Gades, Cádiz (ESP) 12, 20, 91
Gesoriacum, Boulogne (FRA)
  27, 33
Gisacum, Vieil-Evreux (FRA) 14

Hadrumetum, Sousse (TUN) 23
Herculaneum, Herculaneum
  (ITA) 74, 75, 82

Ilici, Elche (ESP) 55
Iuliomagus, Angers (FRA) 35

Juliobona, Lillebonne
  (FRA) 47

Legio, ad Legionem, León,
  Puente Castro (ESP) 56
Leptis Magna, Khoms (LBA)
  47, 64
Liris, Minturno (ITA) 11
Londinium, London (ENG) 28,
  60, 62, 70

Lucus Augusti, Lugo (ESP) 22
Lugdunum, Lyon (FRA) 13, 33, 70, 83
Lugdunum Batavorum, Katwijk aan Zee (NED) 27
Lugdunum Convenae, Saint-Bertrand-de-Comminges (FRA) 25, 73
Luna, Luni (ITA) 11, 63
Lutetia, Paris (FRA) 72

Massalia, Marseille (FRA) 11, 12, 20, 24, 52, 83
Mazaca Cesarea, Kayseri, Eskişehir (TUR) 81
Minatiacum (city of Remi, cf. *Durocortorum*), Nizy-le-Comte (FRA) 46, 53, 59–62, 70, 74
Mosae Traiectum, Maastricht (BEL) 46
Munda, Málaga (province) (ESP) 22

Narbo Martius, Narbonne (FRA) 25, 33, 53
Nemausus, Nîmes (FRA) 13, 36, 63, 70, 85, 89
Nikaïa, Nice (FRA) 21, 34
Noviomagus, Neumagen, city of Treveri, cf. *Augusta Treuerorum* (GER) 46

Olisipo, Lisbon (POR) 33
Ostia, Ostia (ITA) 11, 61

Palma, Palma de Mallorca (ESP) 21
Pergamum, Pergamon (TUR) 48
Phoebiana, Faimingen (GER) 14
Pollentia, Alcudia (de Pollença) (ESP) 21
Pompeii, Pompeii (ITA) 47, 61, 75
Portus Herculis Monoecus, Monaco (MON) 55

Portus Ilicitanus, Santa Pola (ESP) 21, 55
Portus Namnetorum, Condeuincum, Nantes (FRA) 33, 56
Portus Pictonum, Ratiatum, Rezé (FRA) 33
Puteoli, Pozzuoli (ITA) 11

Ratae Corieltauorum, Leicester (ENG) 73
Ravenna, Ravenna (ITA) 84
Roma, Rome (ITA) 1, 9, 19, 33, 45, 60, 68, 79, 87

Sabratha, Az Zawiya (district) (LBA) 47
Saguntum, Sagunto (ESP) 73, 91
Samarobriua, Amiens (FRA) 33
Segobriga, Saelices (ESP) 55, 70
Sitifis, Setif (ALG) 73
Smyrna, Izmir (TUR) 48

Tarraco, Tarragona (ESP) 13, 55, 63, 84
Termes, Montejo de Tiermes (ESP) 70
Thamugadi, Timgad (ALG) 19
Thysdrus, El Djem (TUN) 23
Tipasa, Tipaza (ALG) 61
Tolosa, Toulouse (FRA) 33, 64
Tyrus, Tyre (LBN) 20, 23

Ucubi, Espejo (ESP) 60
Urso, Osuna (ESP) 74

Valentia, Valencia (ESP) 21, 22
Venta Silurum, Caerwent (WAL) 70
Vienna, Vienna (FRA) 72
Vindolanda, Chesterholm (ENG) 56
Volubilis, Meknes (prefecture) (MAR) 61

For Product Safety Concerns and Information please contact our EU representative GPSR@taylorandfrancis.com
Taylor & Francis Verlag GmbH, Kaufingerstraße 24, 80331 München, Germany

www.ingramcontent.com/pod-product-compliance
Lightning Source LLC
Chambersburg PA
CBHW070848160426
43192CB00012B/2348